A DAY AT THE CIRCUS

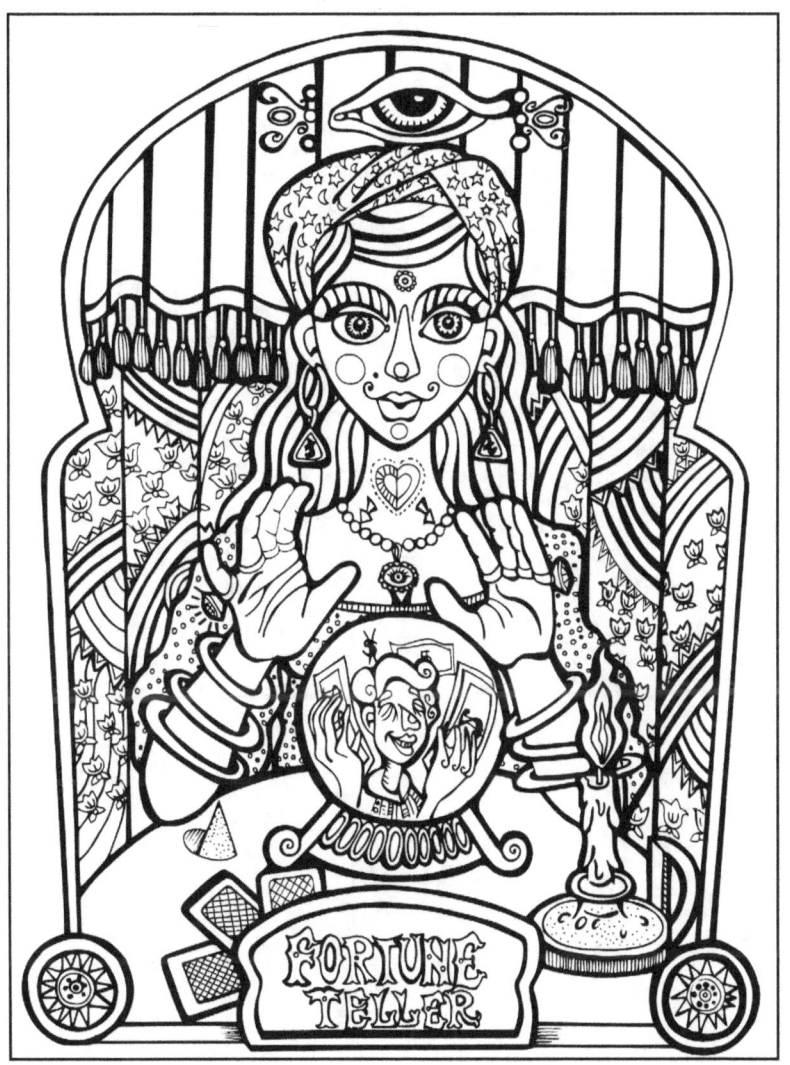

Introduction to "A Day at the Circus"

Luciana Guerra is a talented and highly respected artist living in Buenos Aires, Argentina. Since graduating with a degree in Fine Arts from the National University of Rosario in 2001, Luciana has continually refined her artistic skills. Her exceptional versatility and creativity have allowed her to excel while completing a wide variety of projects as a freelance artist.

The 40 illustrations that Luciana created for this book demonstrate her ability to capture the essence of the magical experience provided by a circus. We find clowns, magicians, jugglers, fortune tellers, trapeze artists, strongmen, knife throwers, Siamese twins and gymnasts as well as lions, tigers, horses, monkeys, bears and all the other animals typically found at the circus.

Luciana's illustrations will liberate the inner child in residing in each of us and they will virtually transport us to the magical world of the circus.

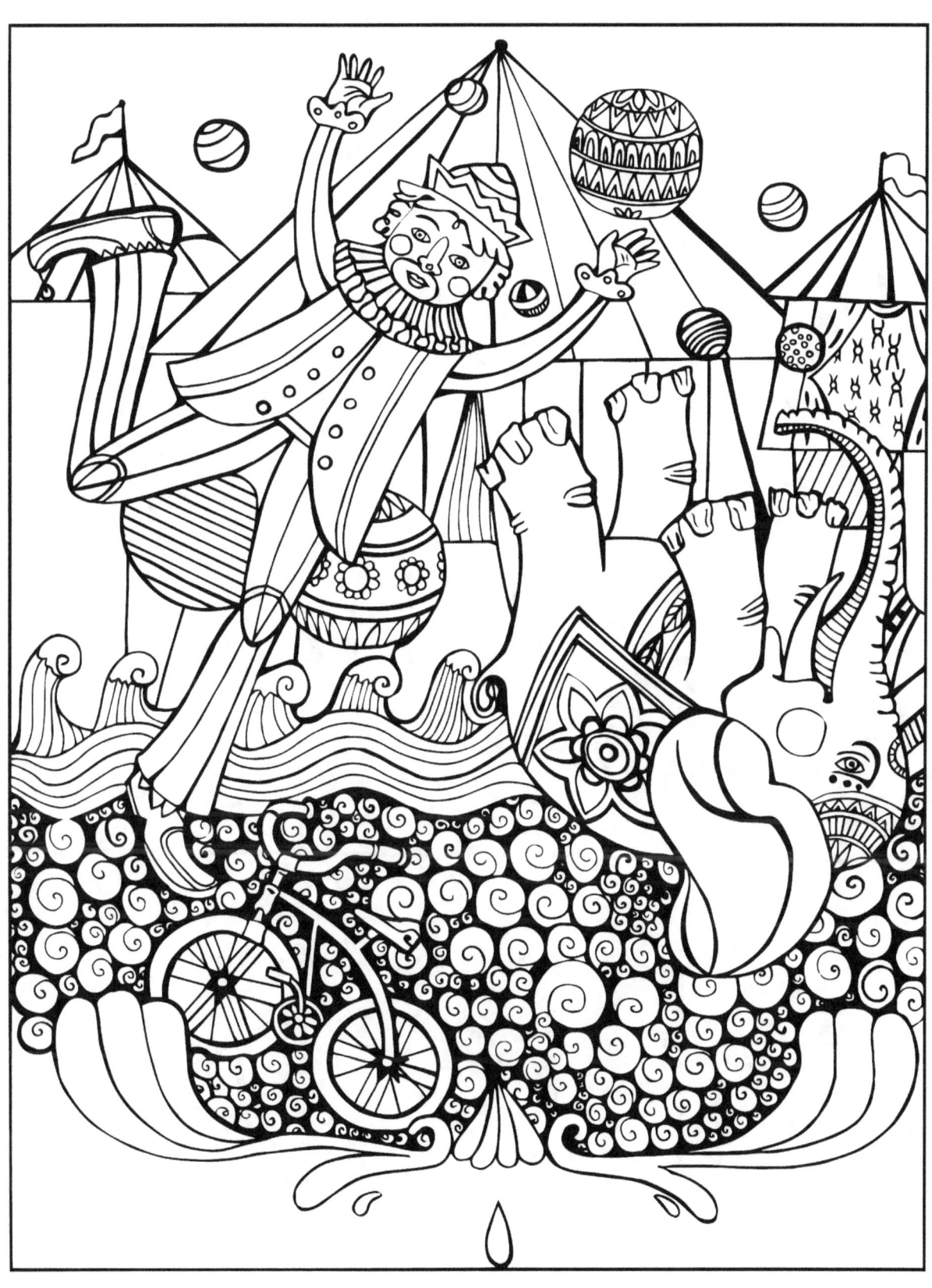

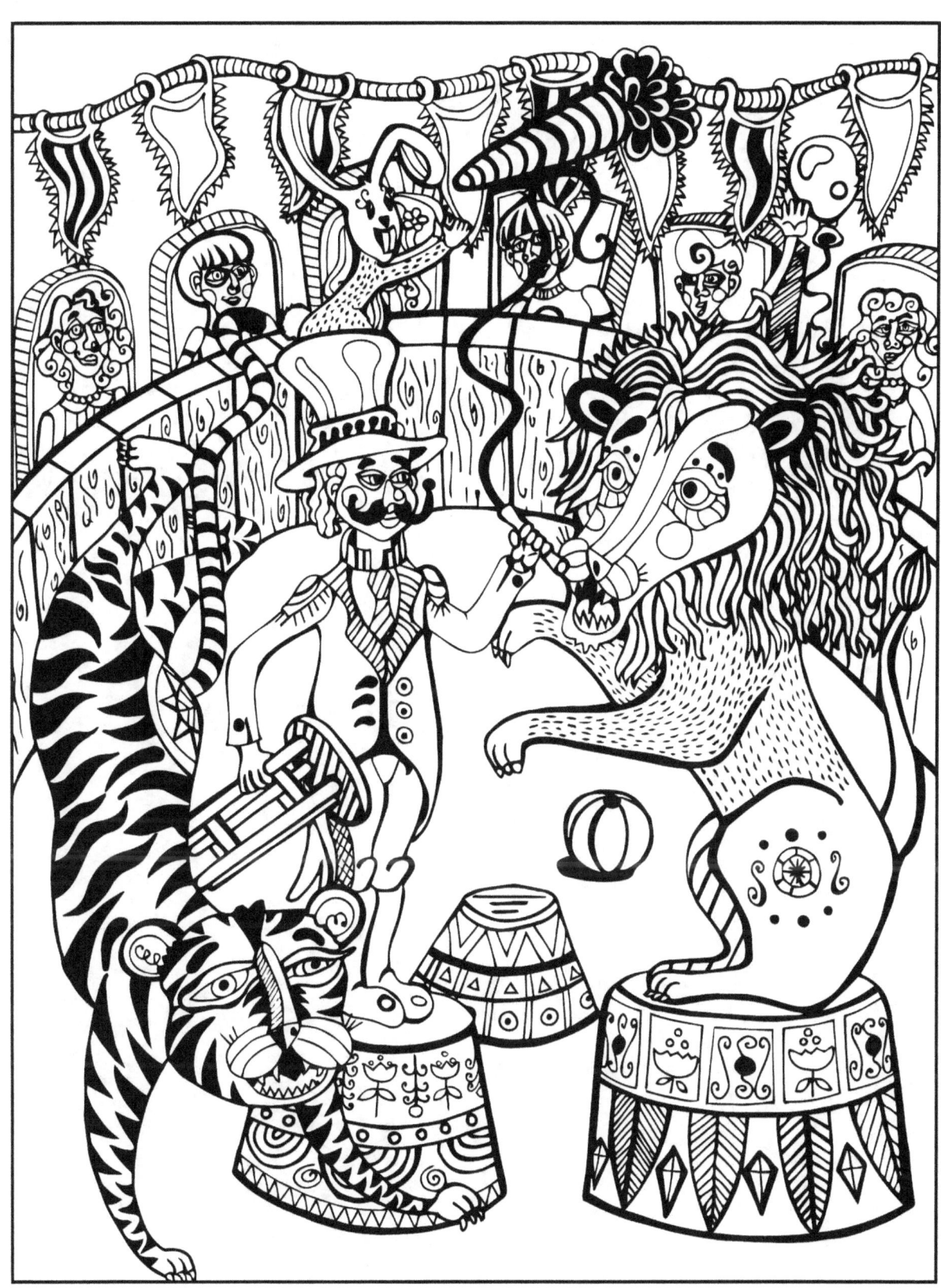

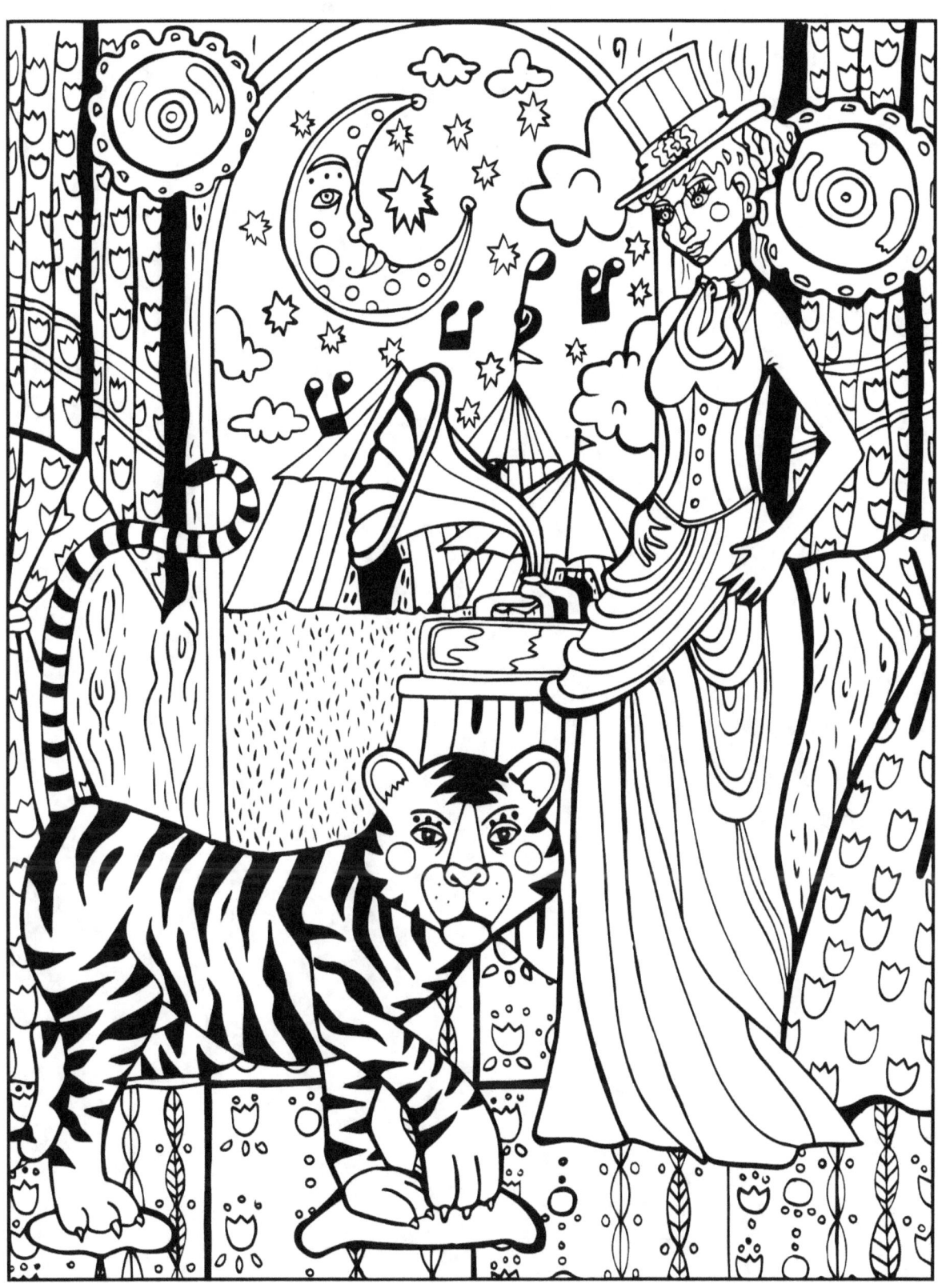

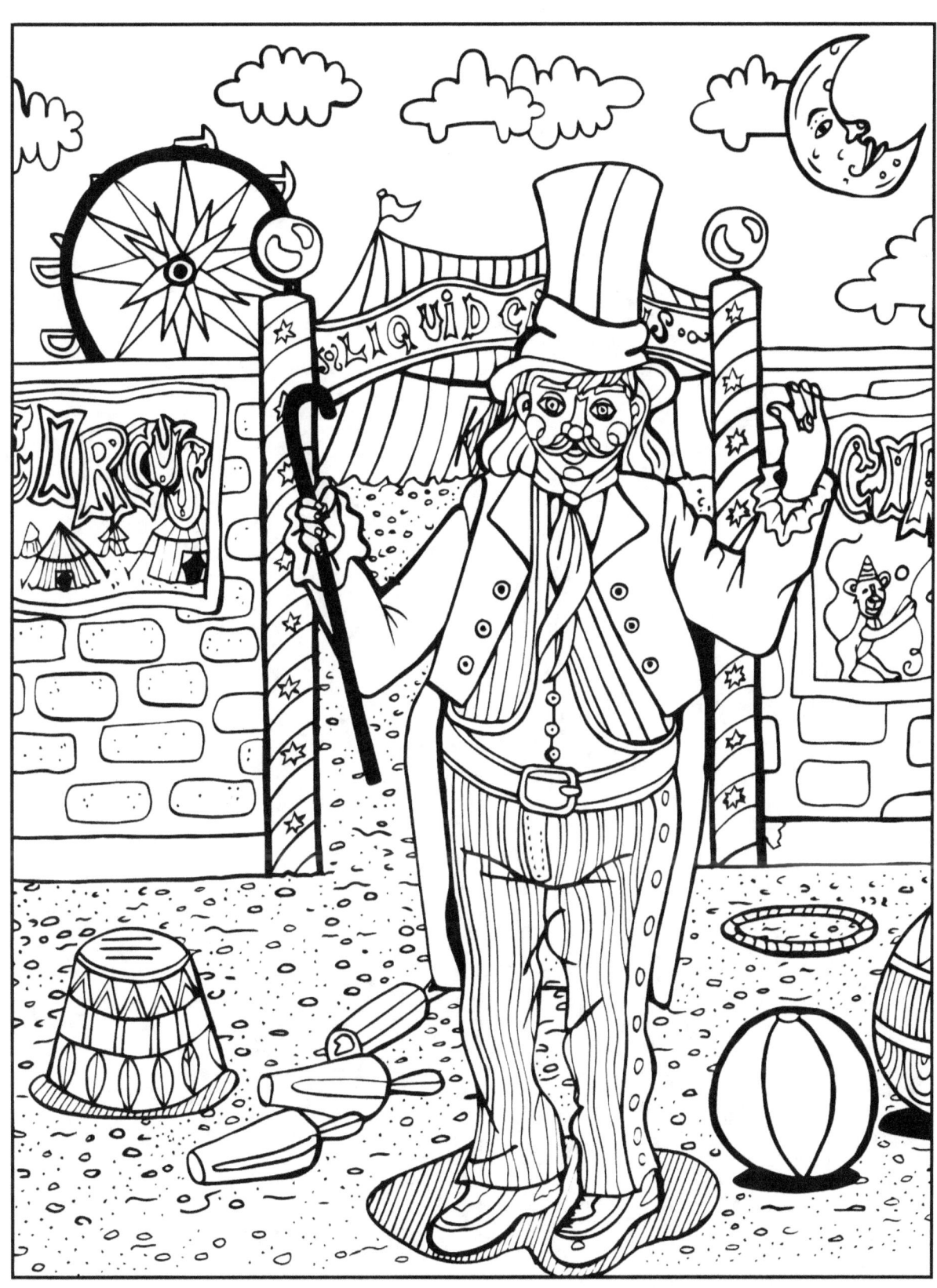

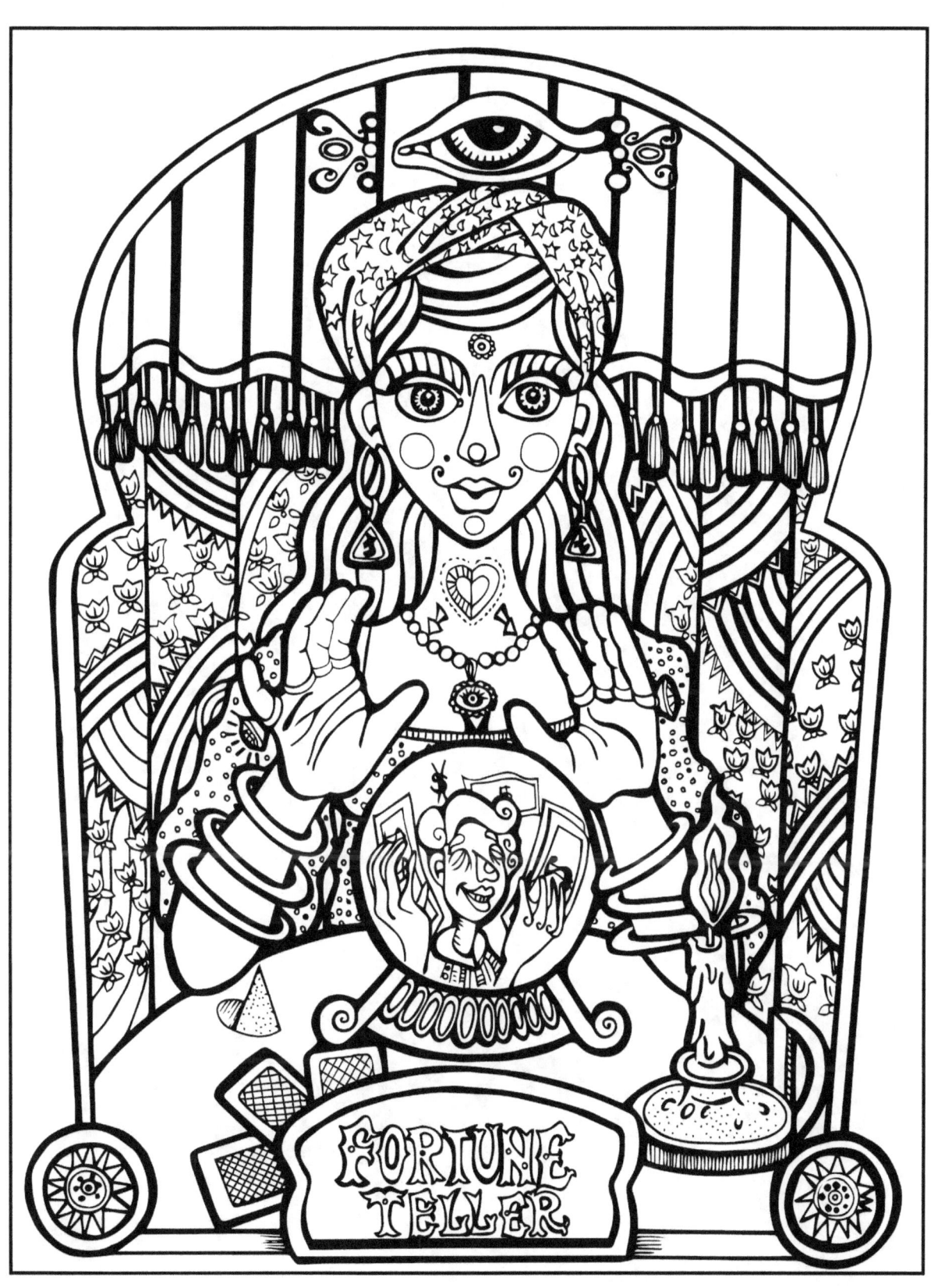

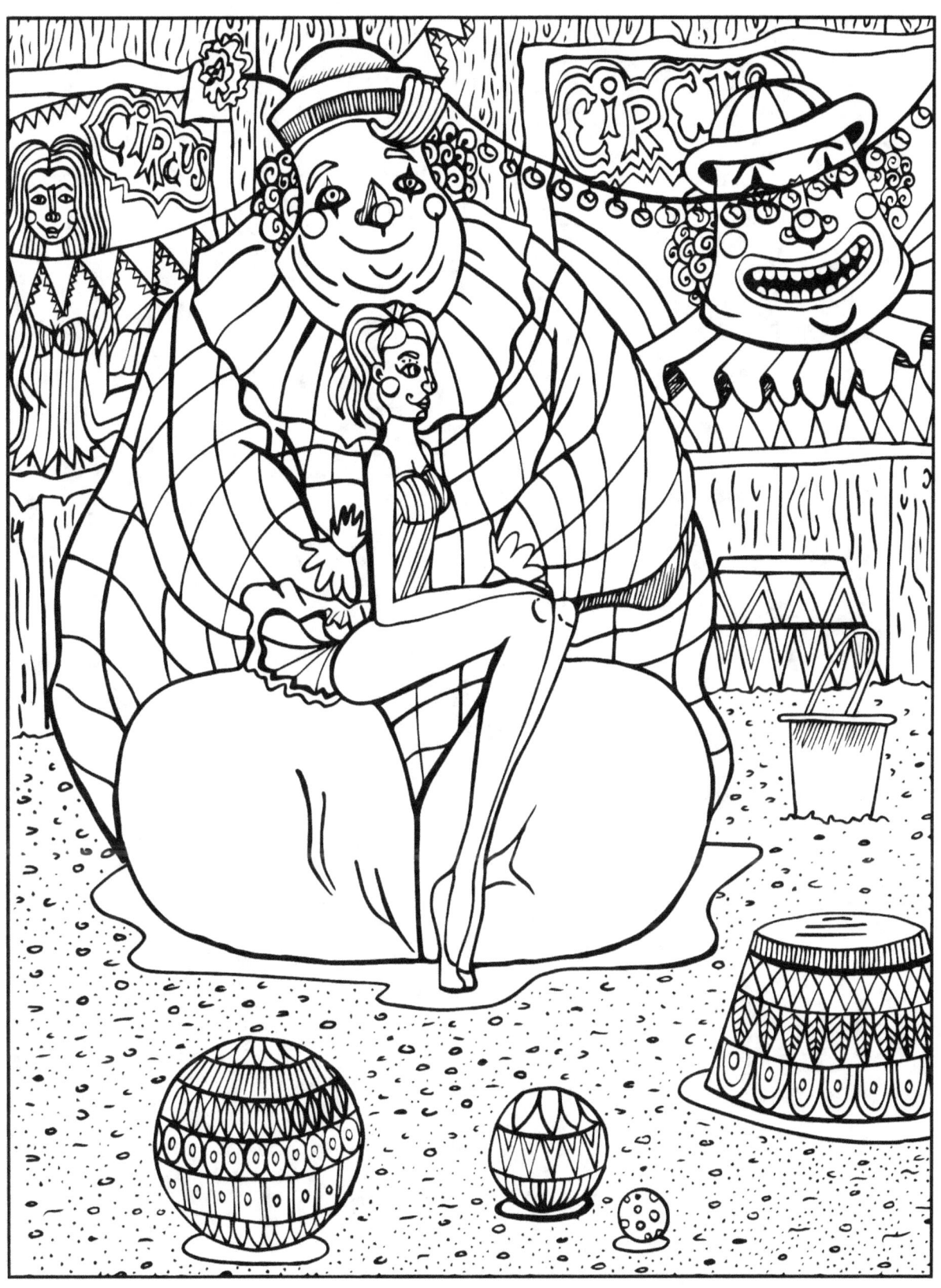

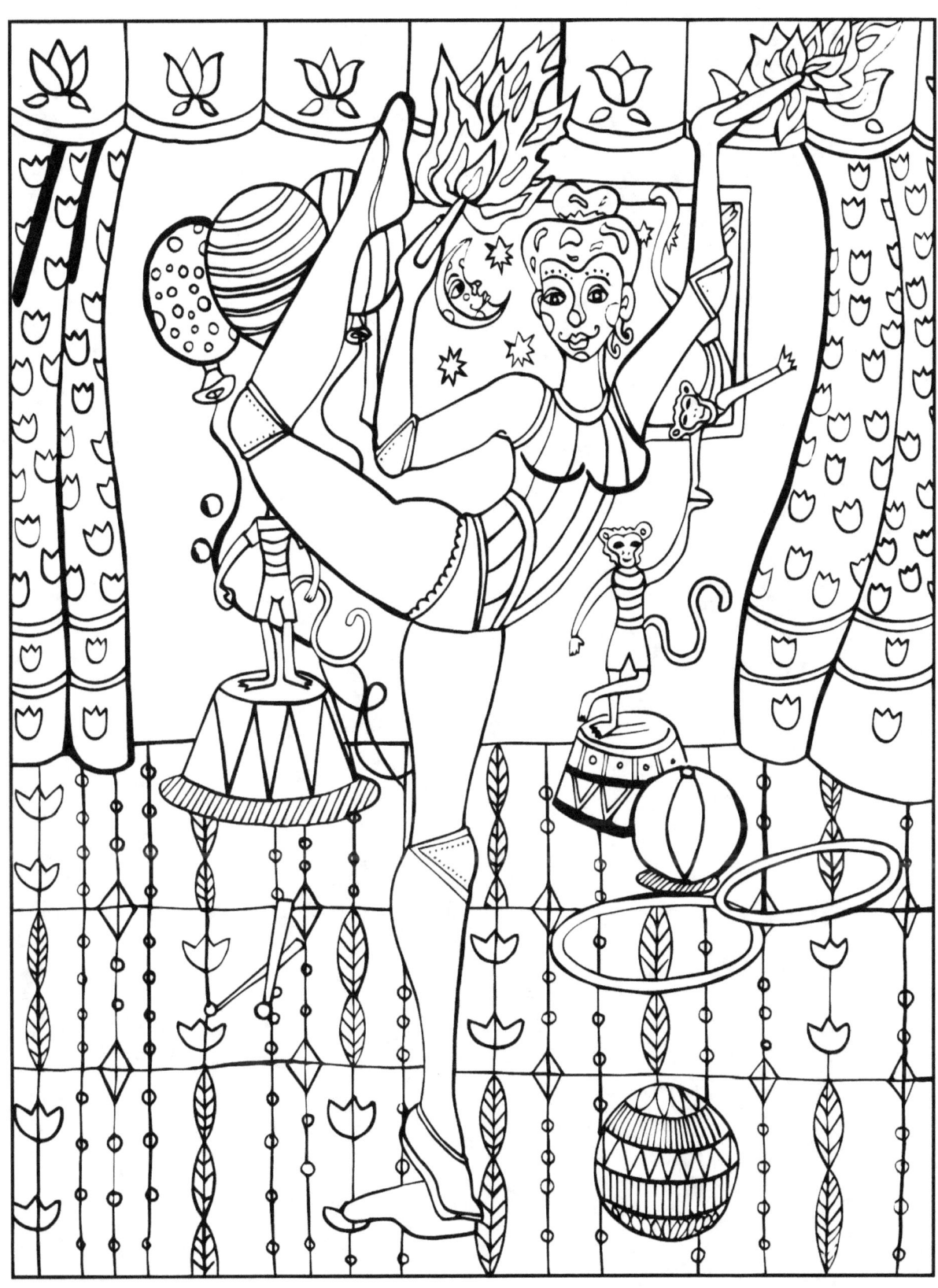

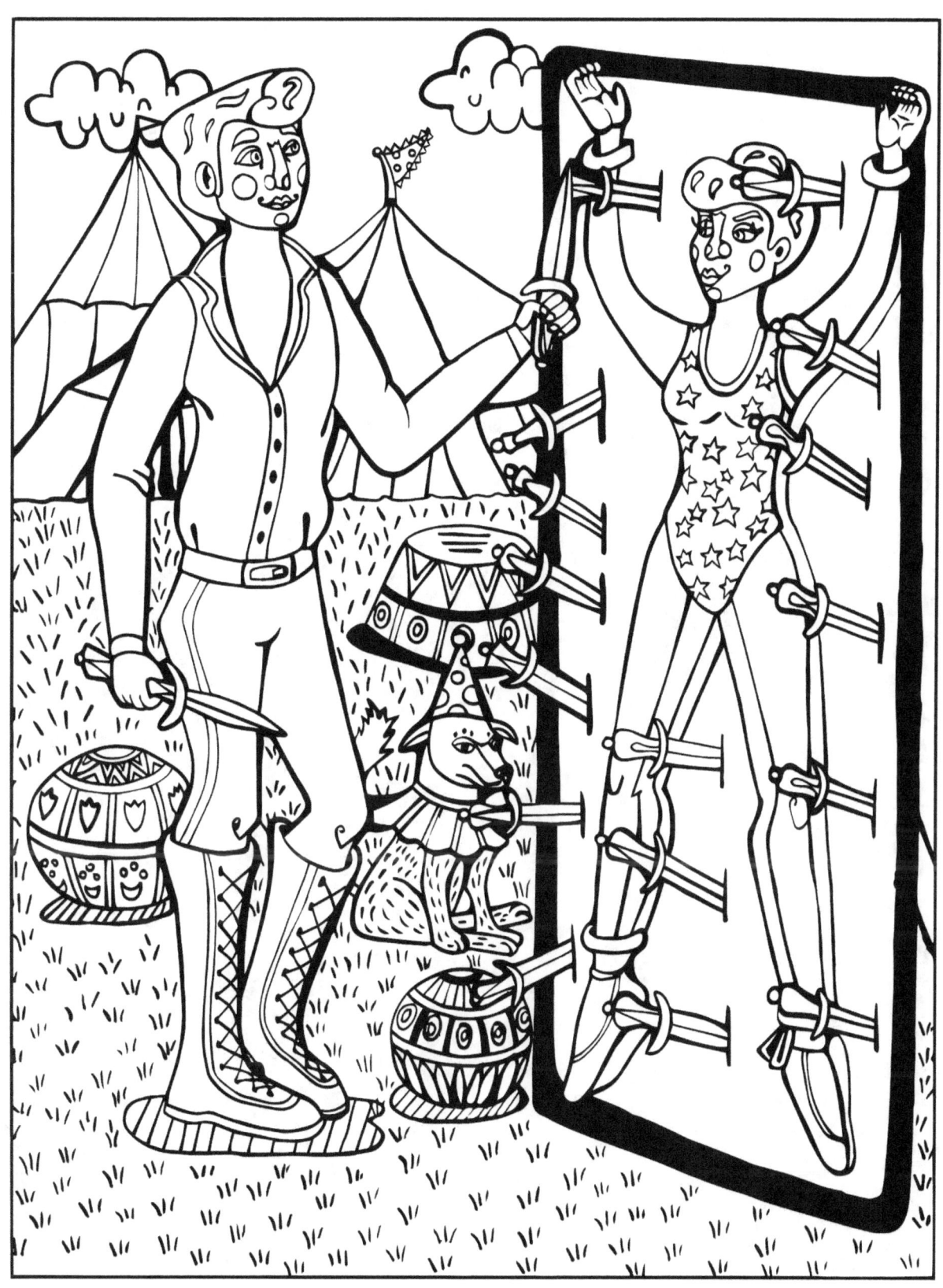

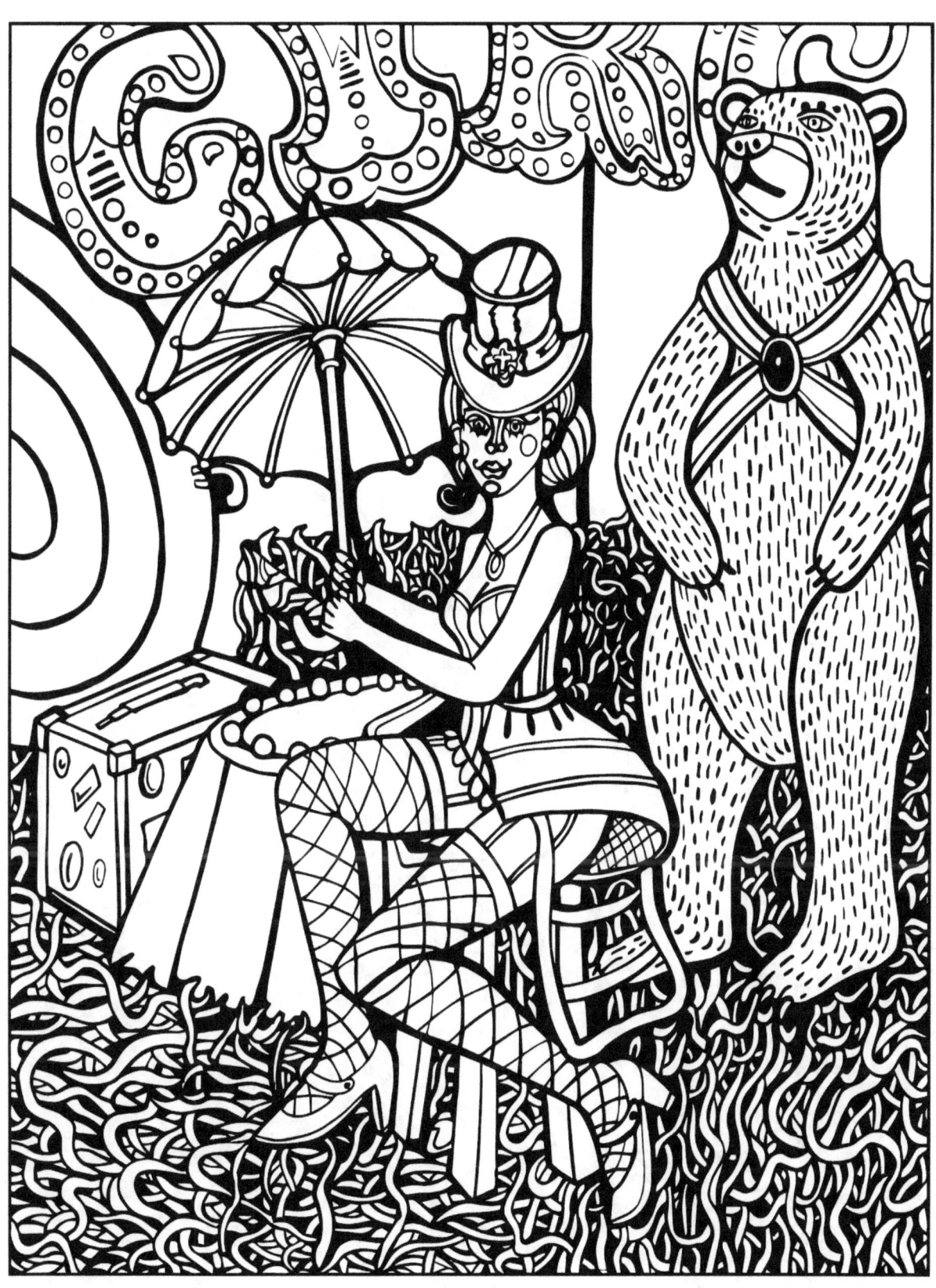

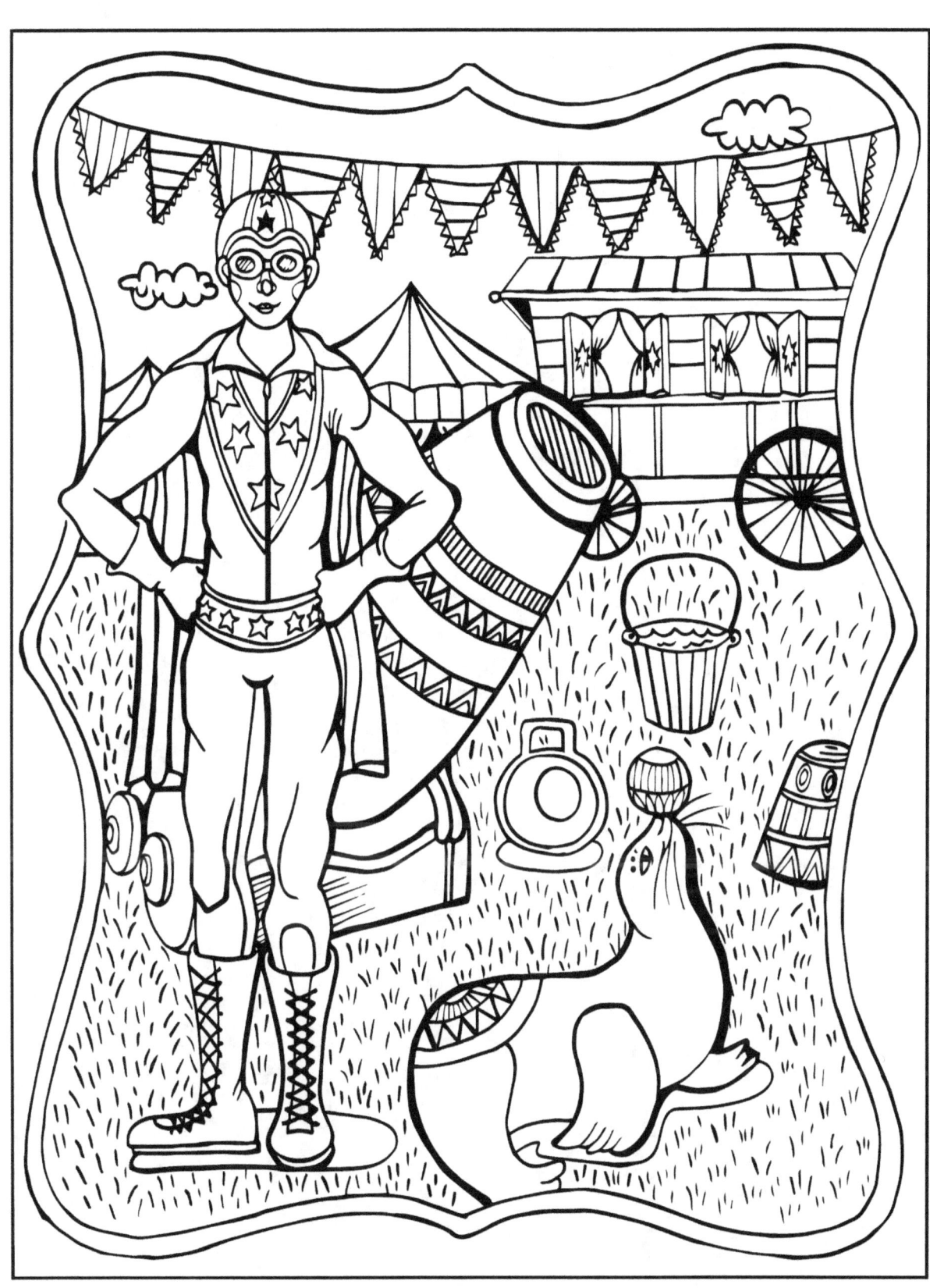

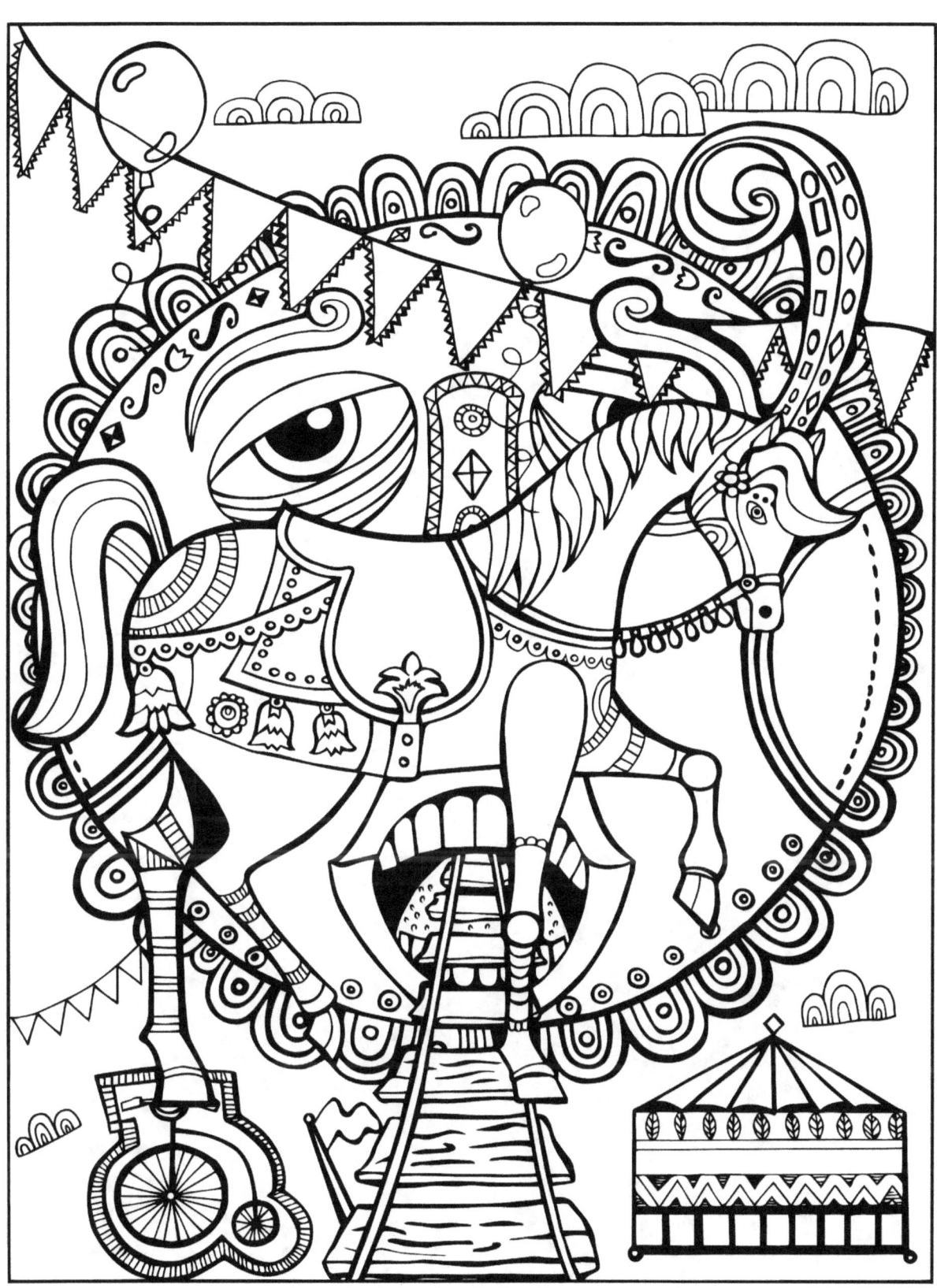

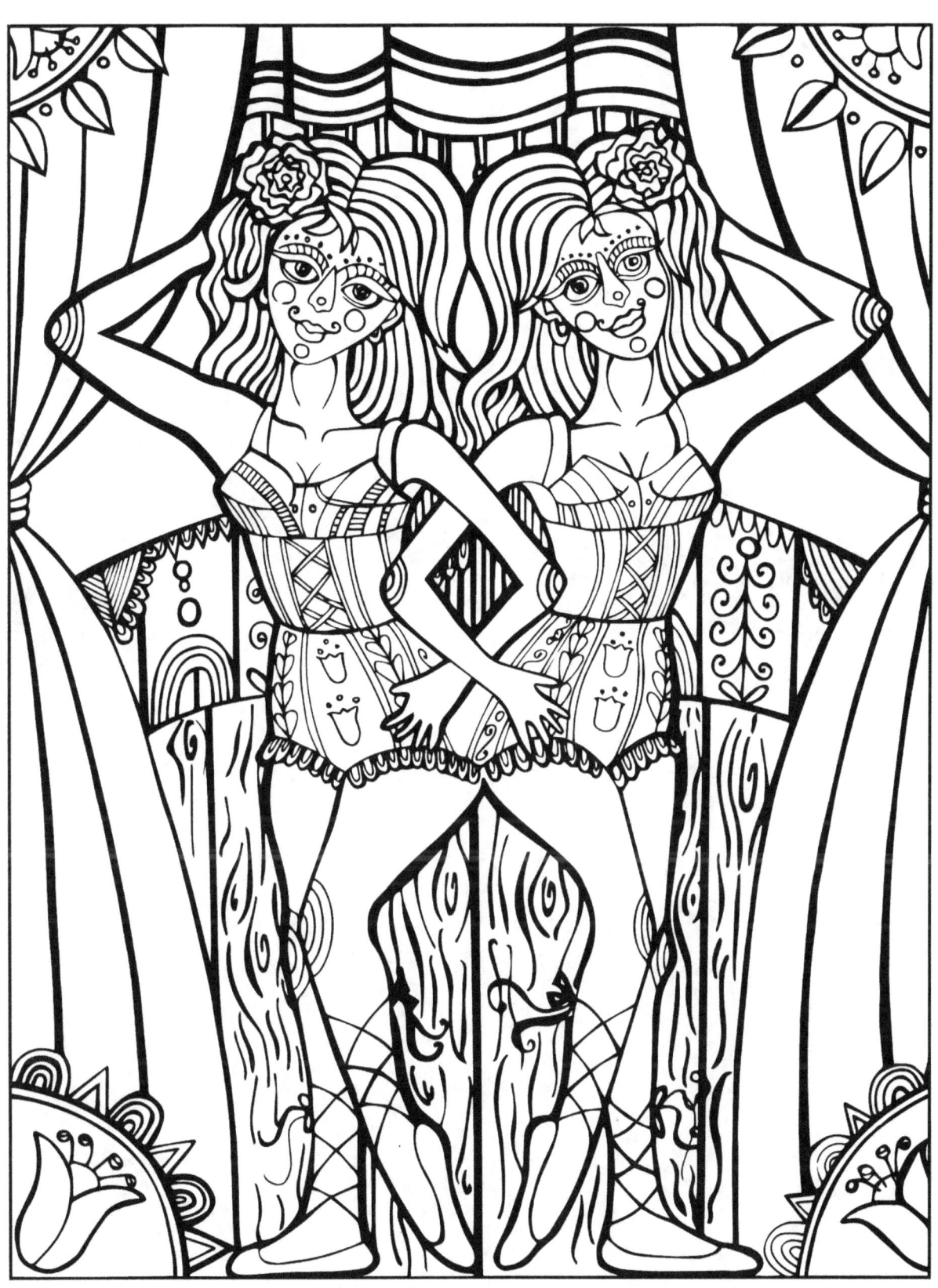

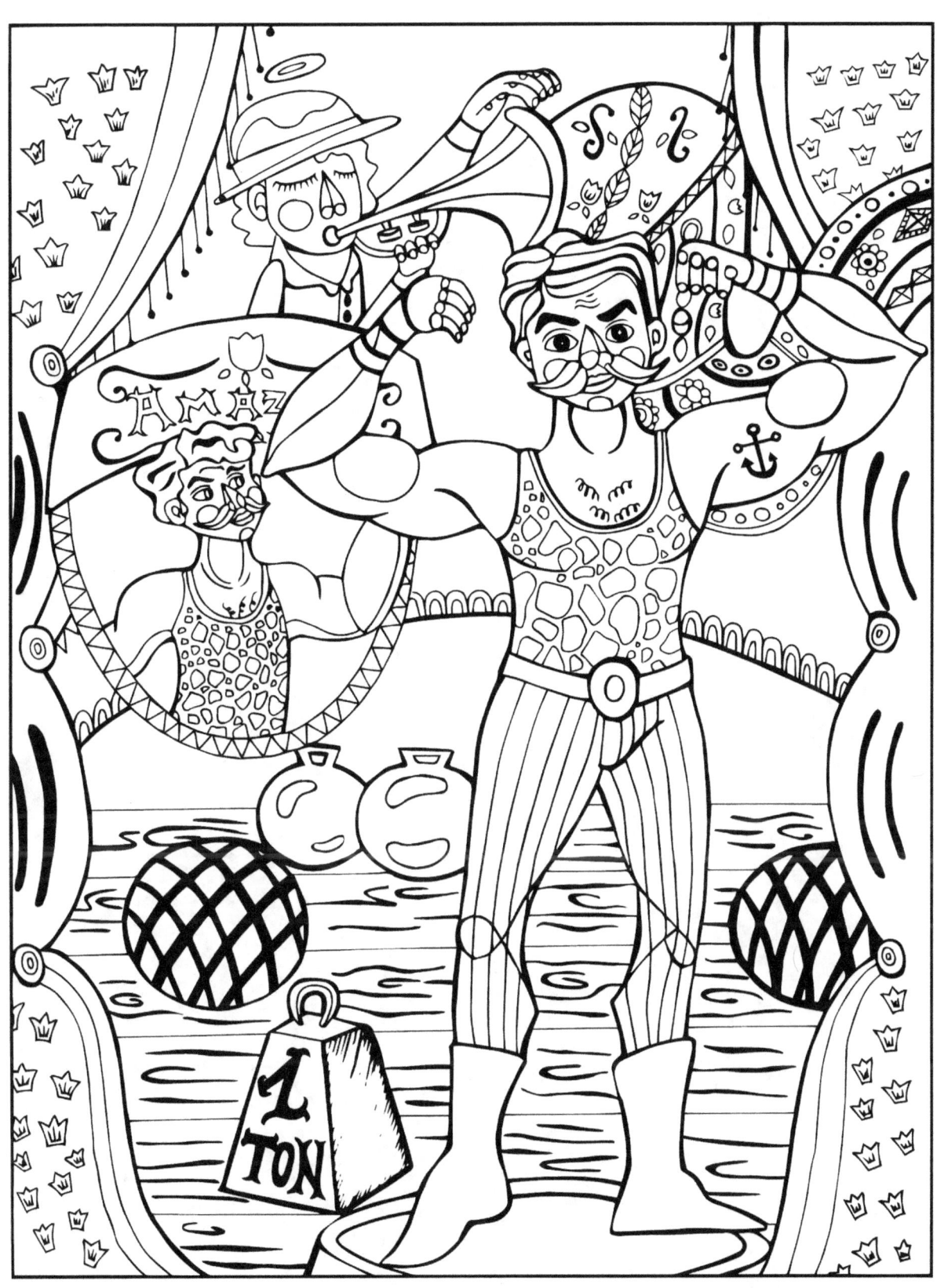

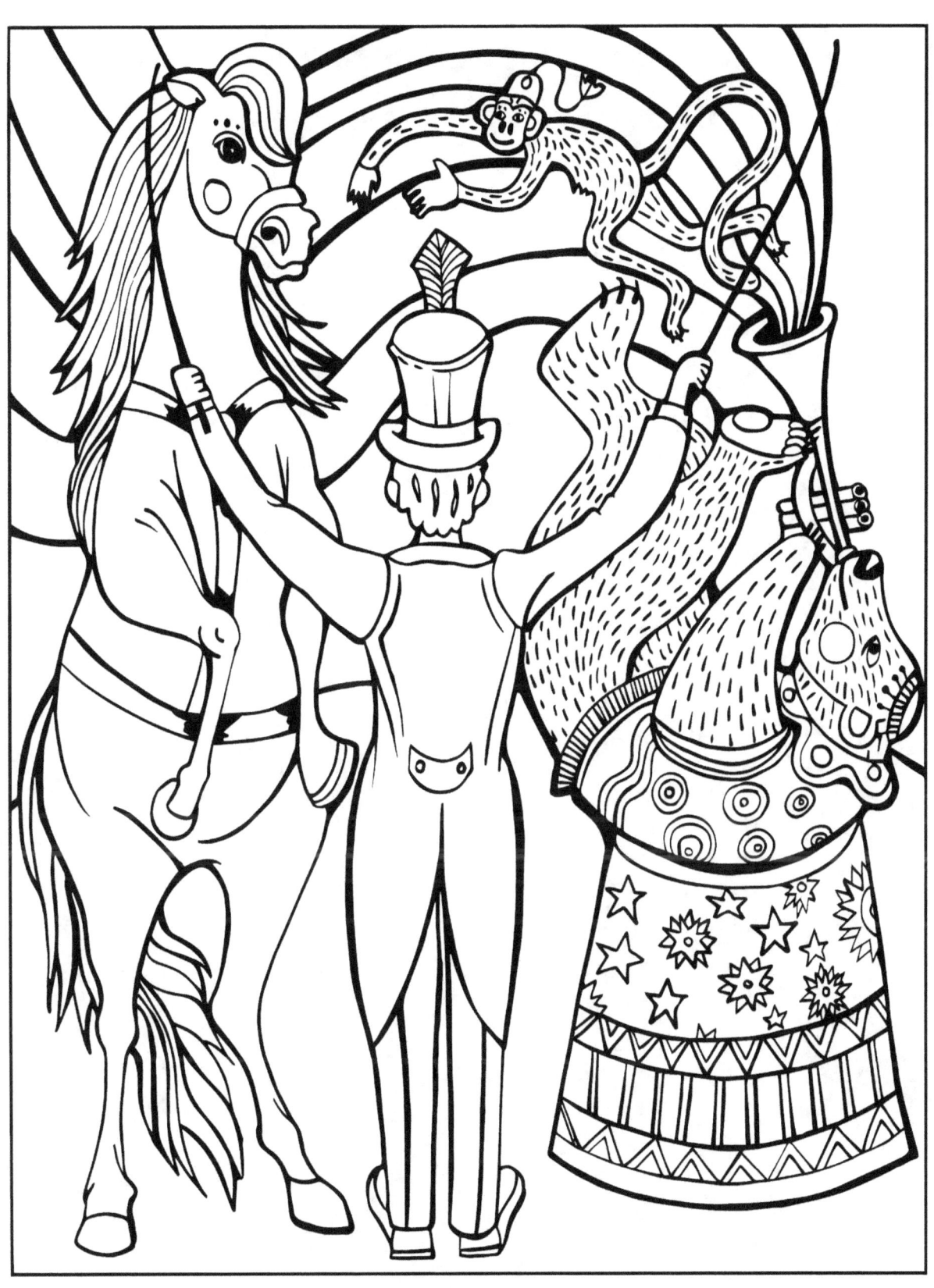

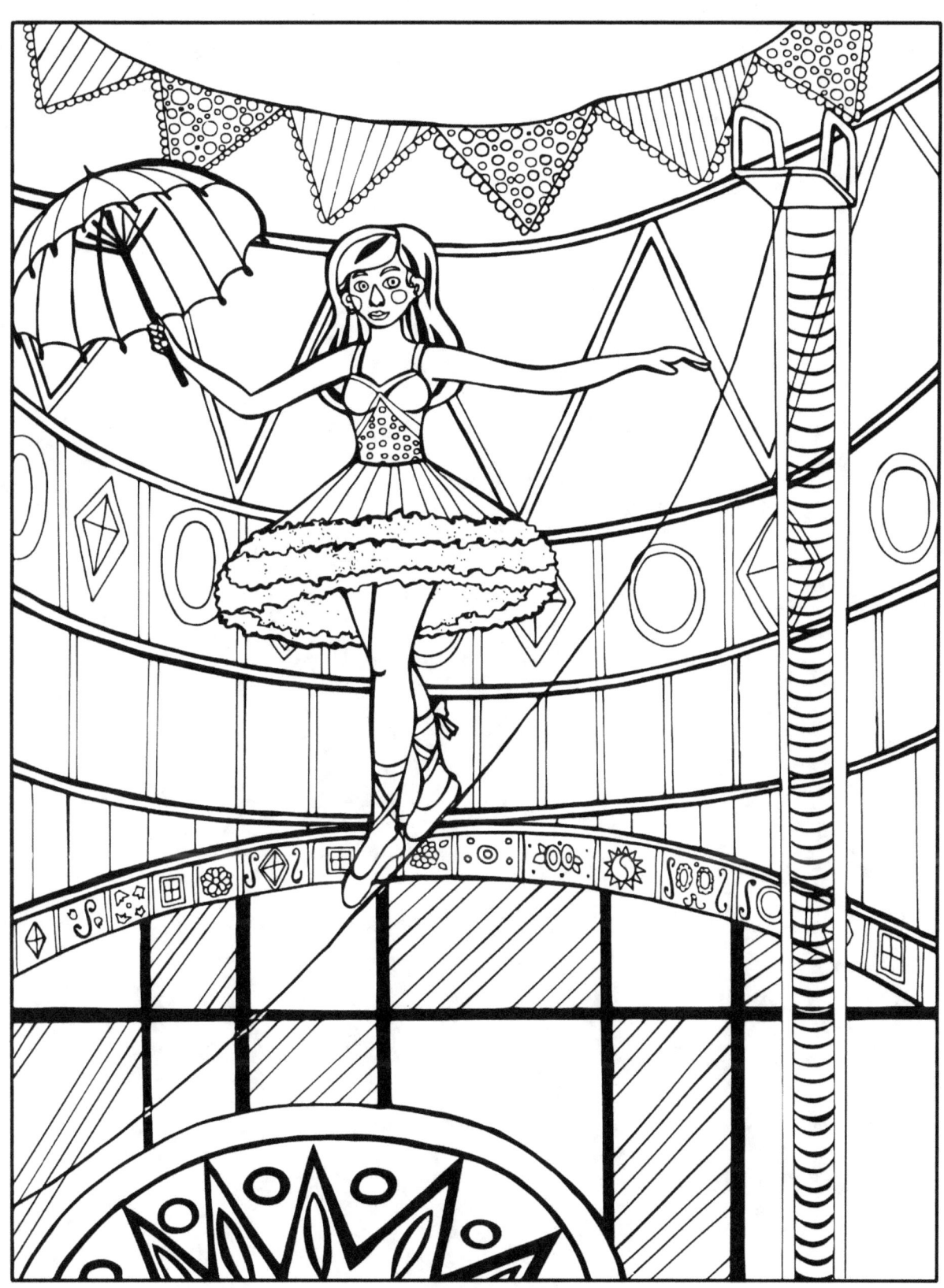

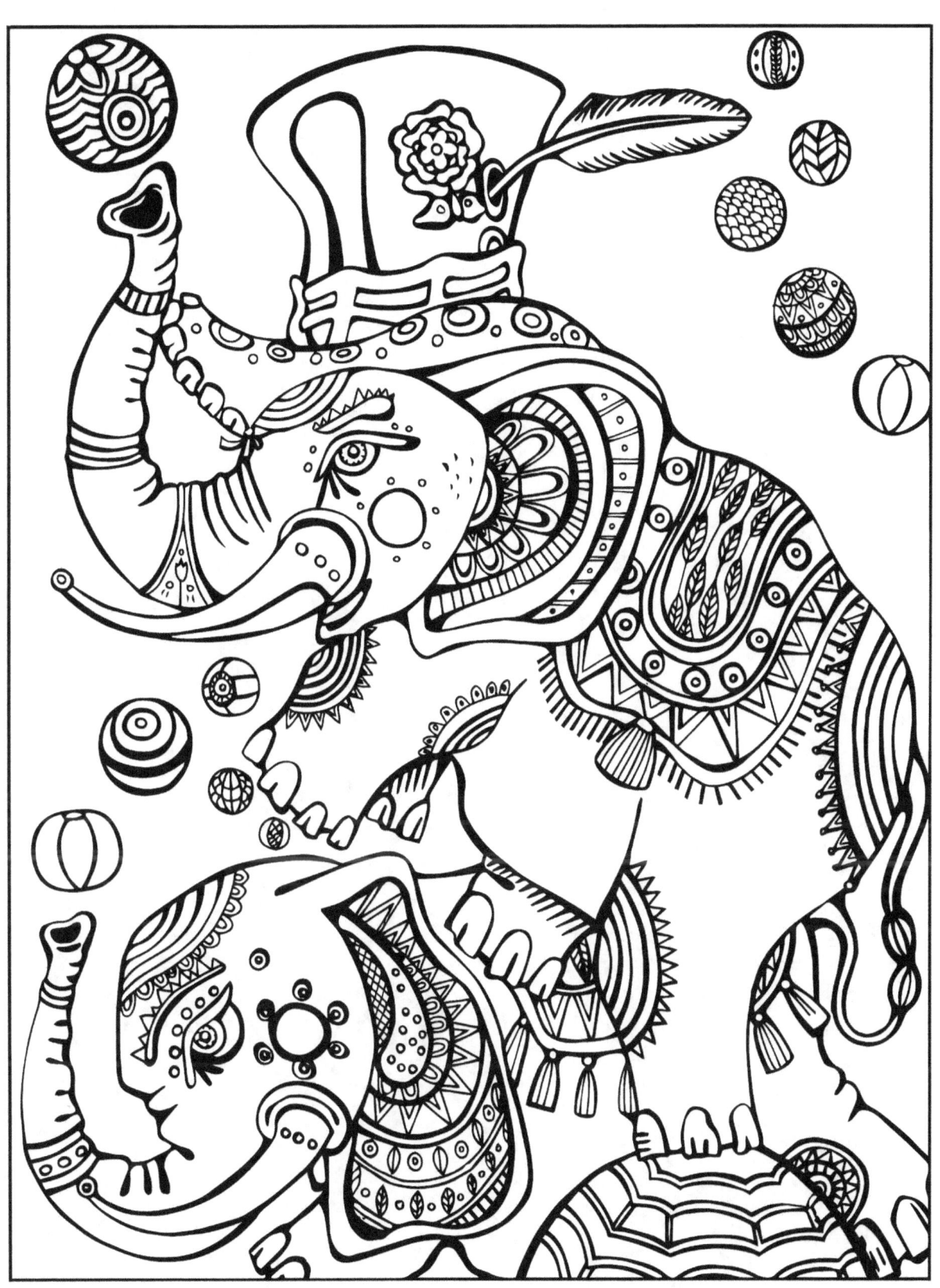

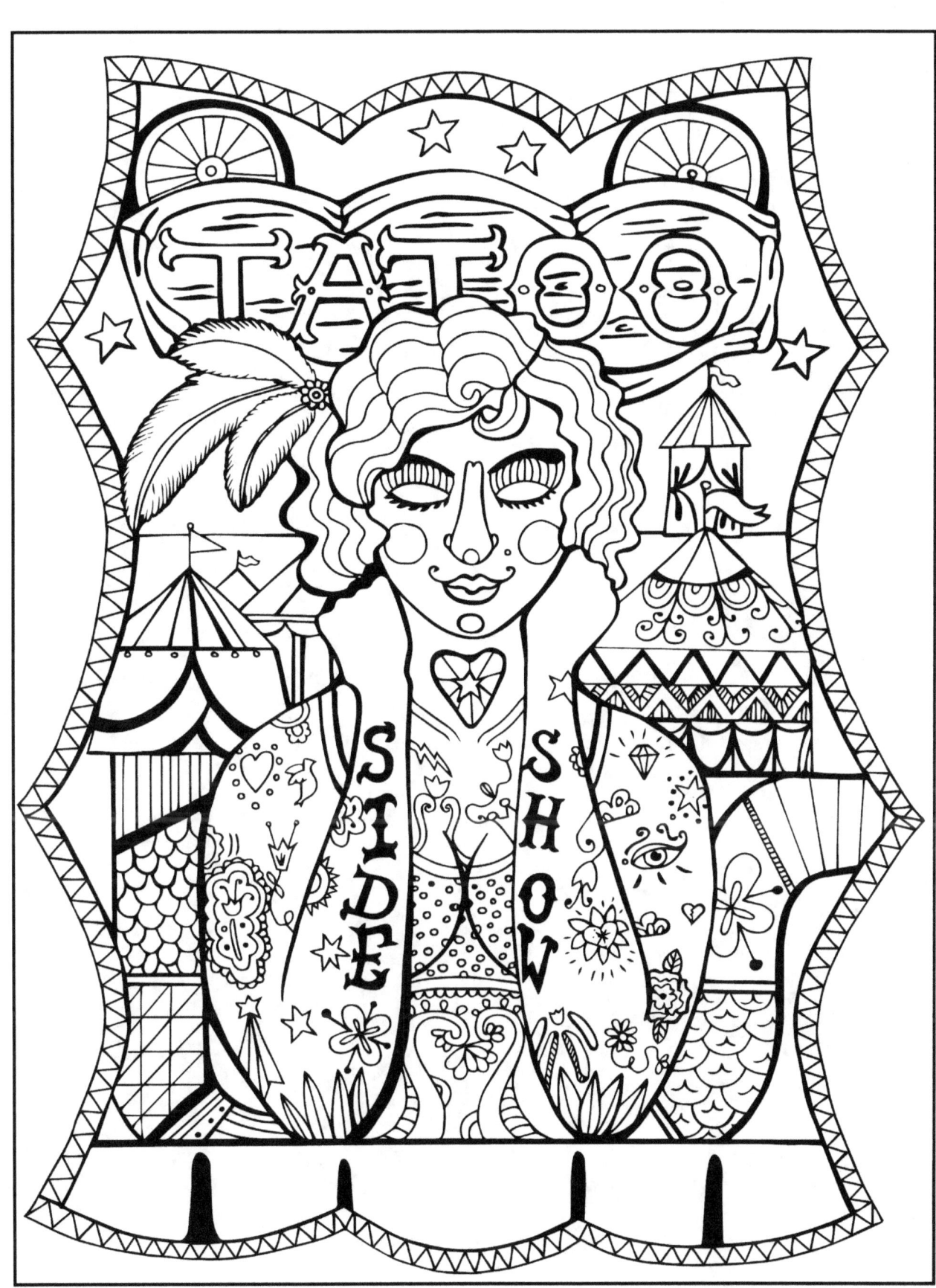

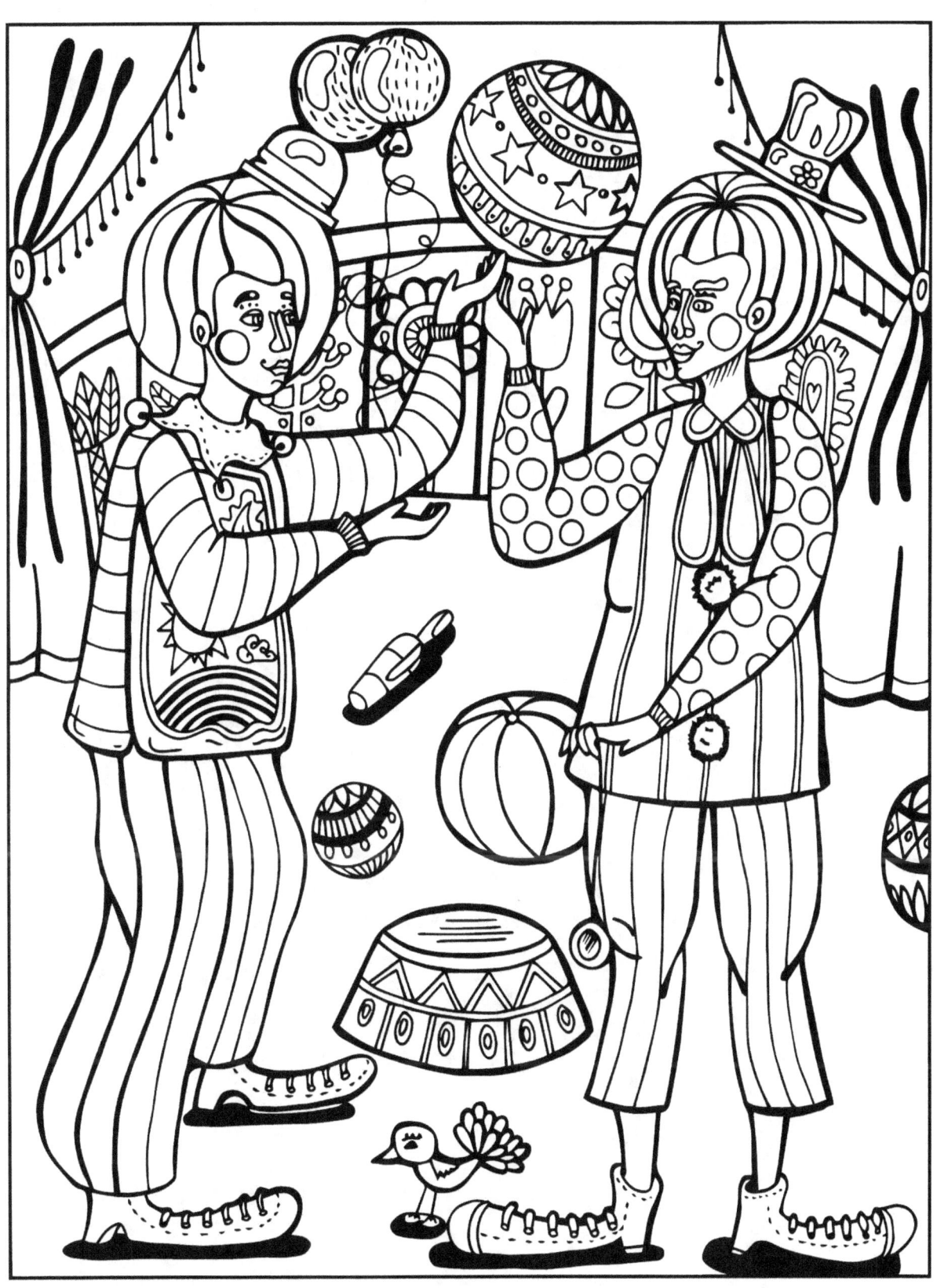

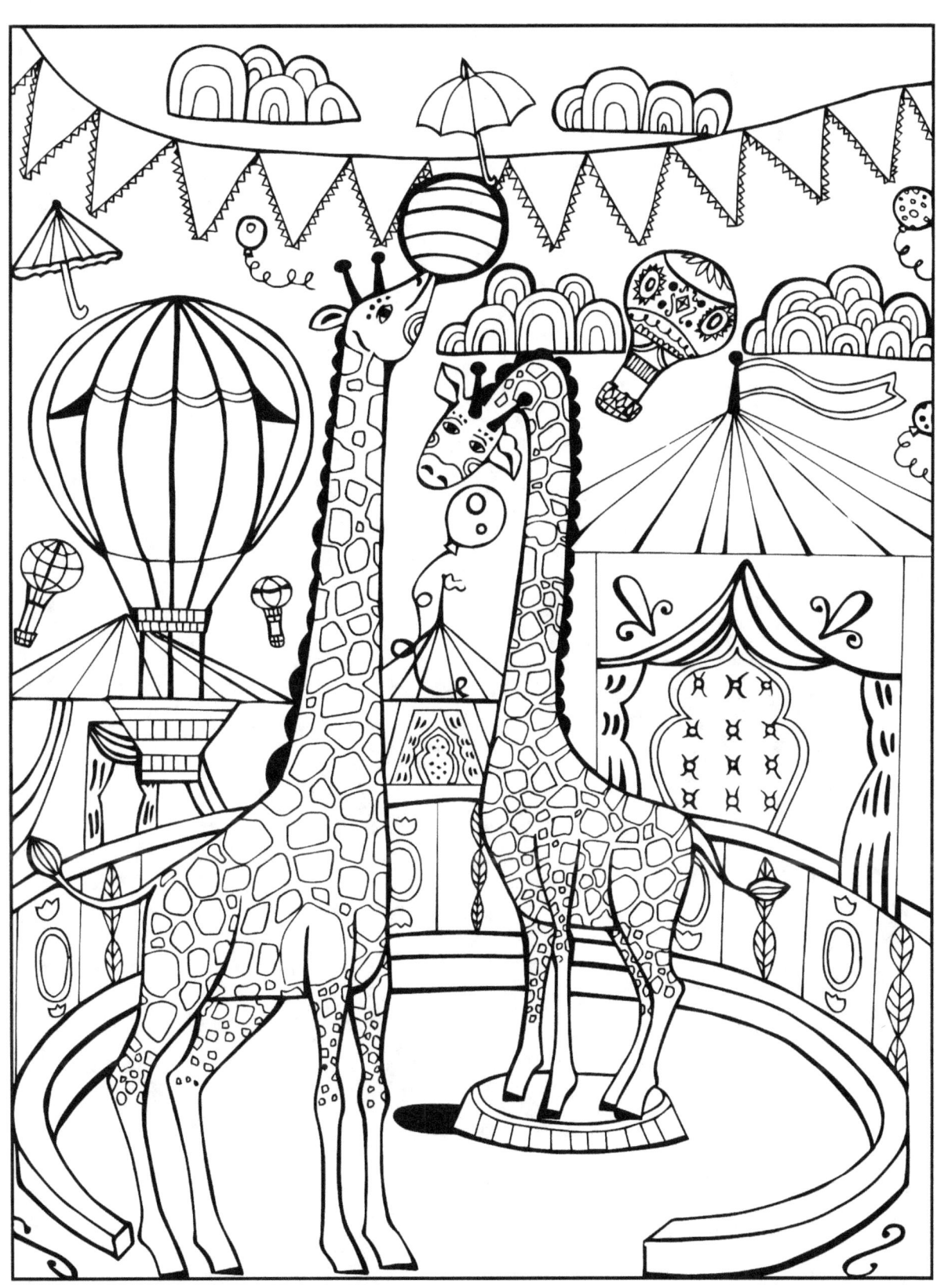

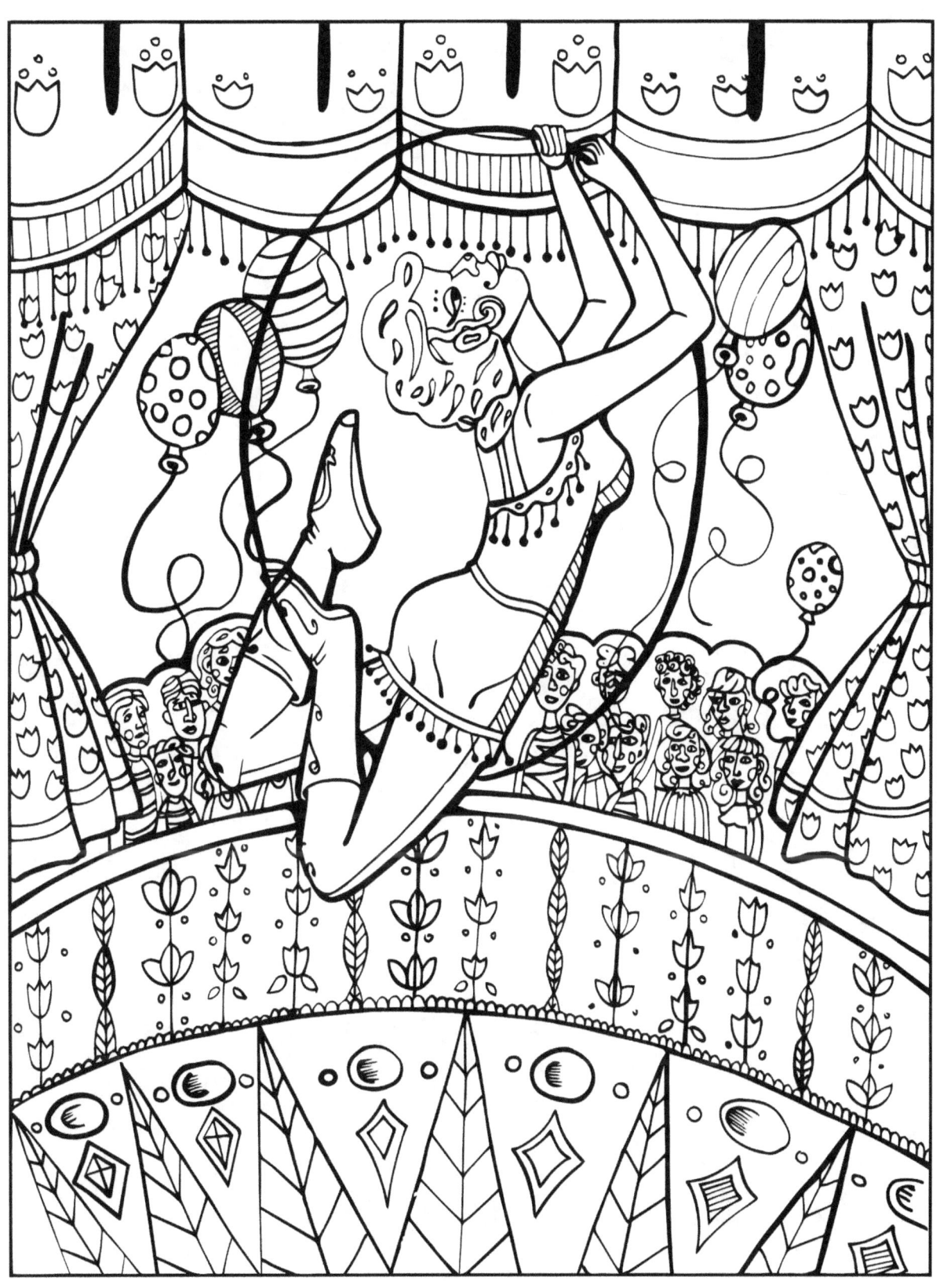

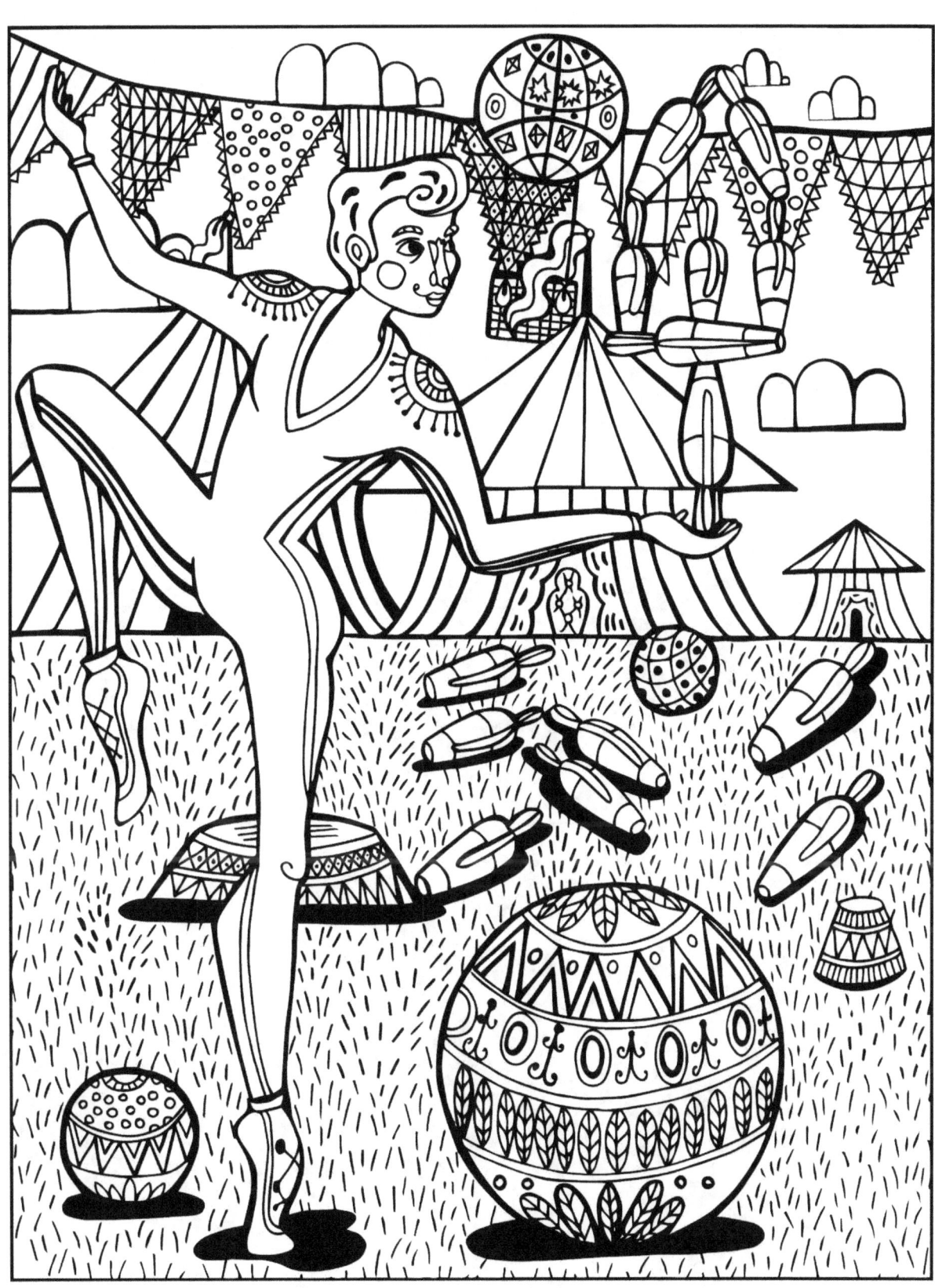

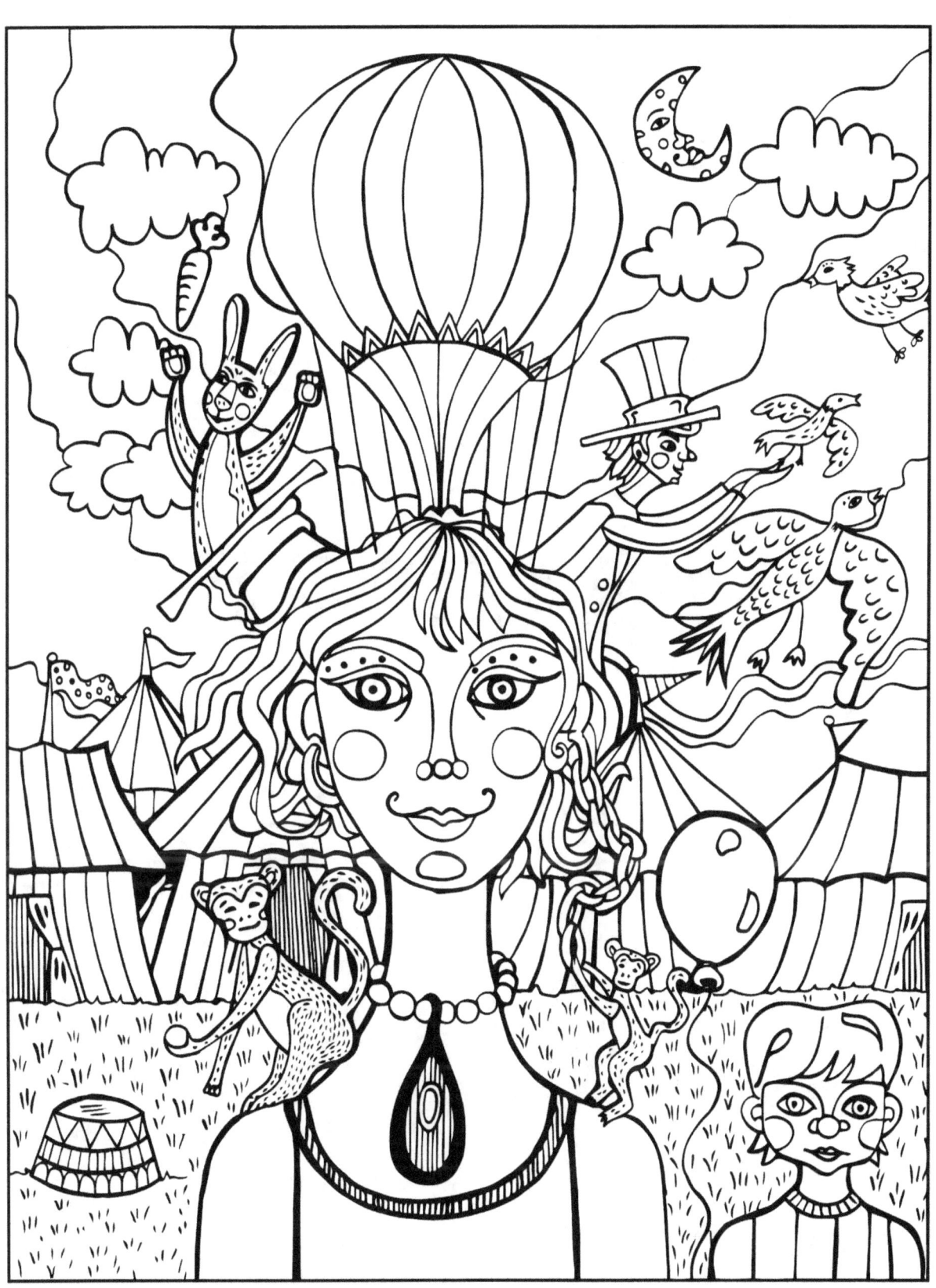

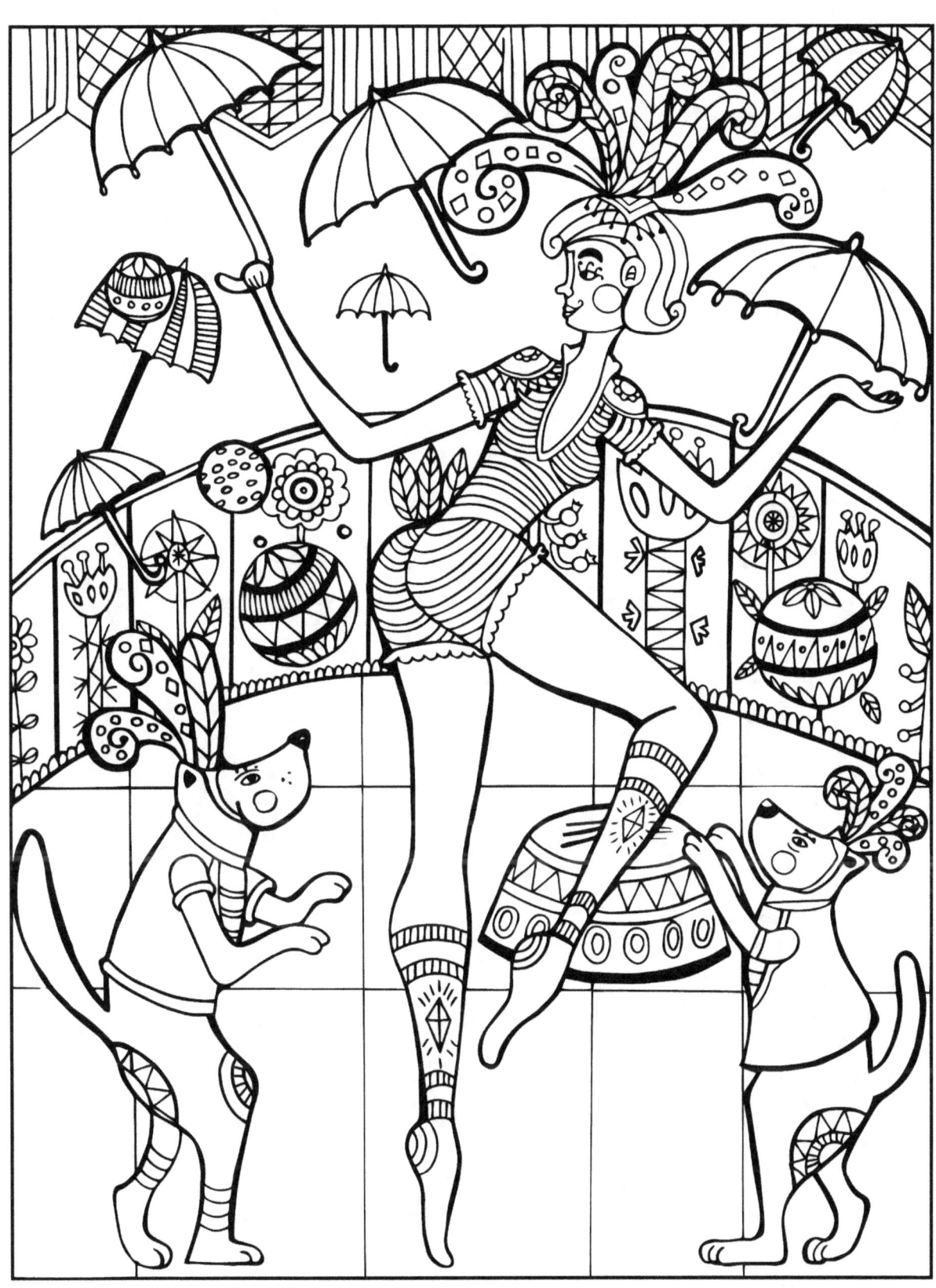

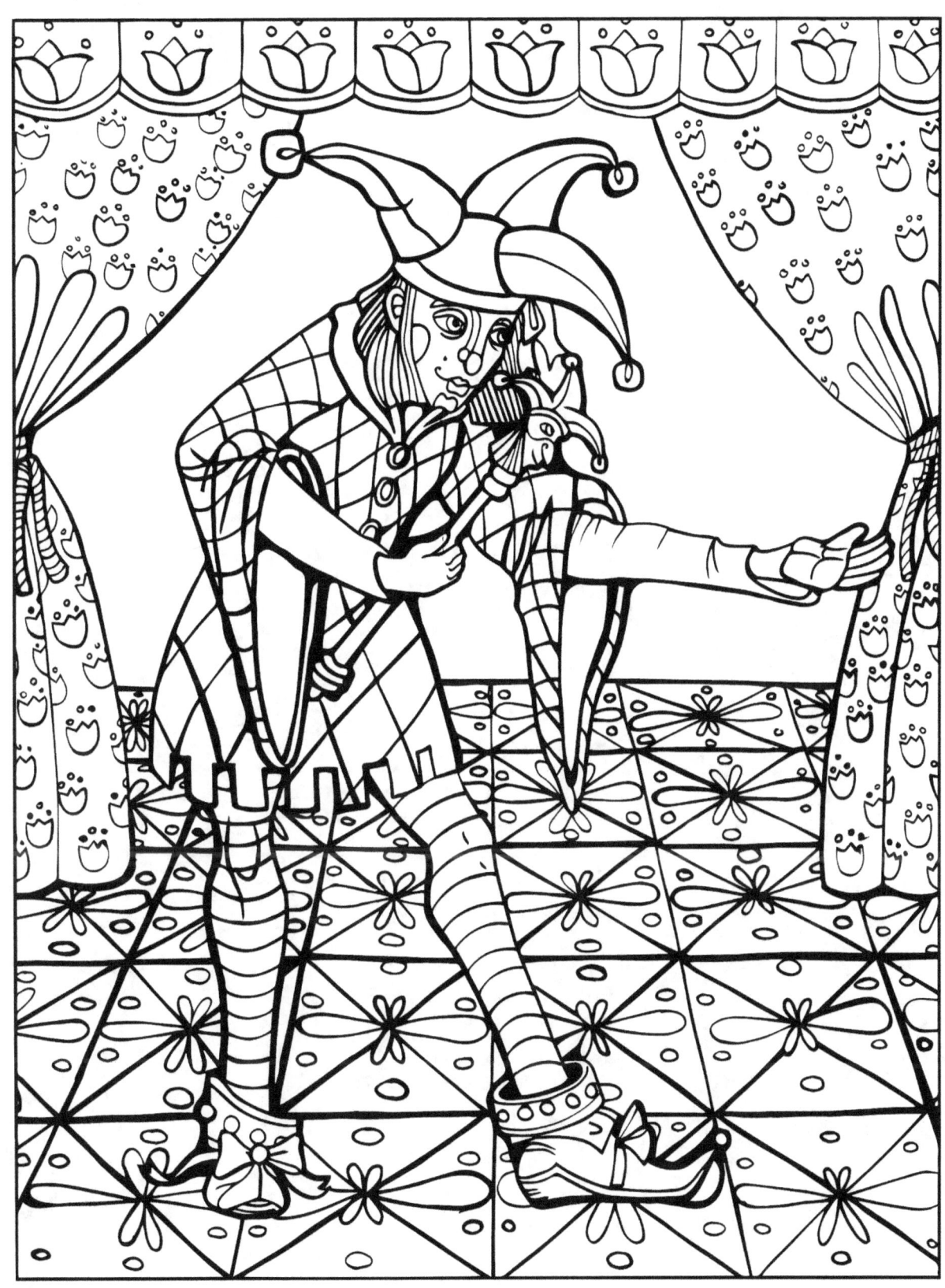

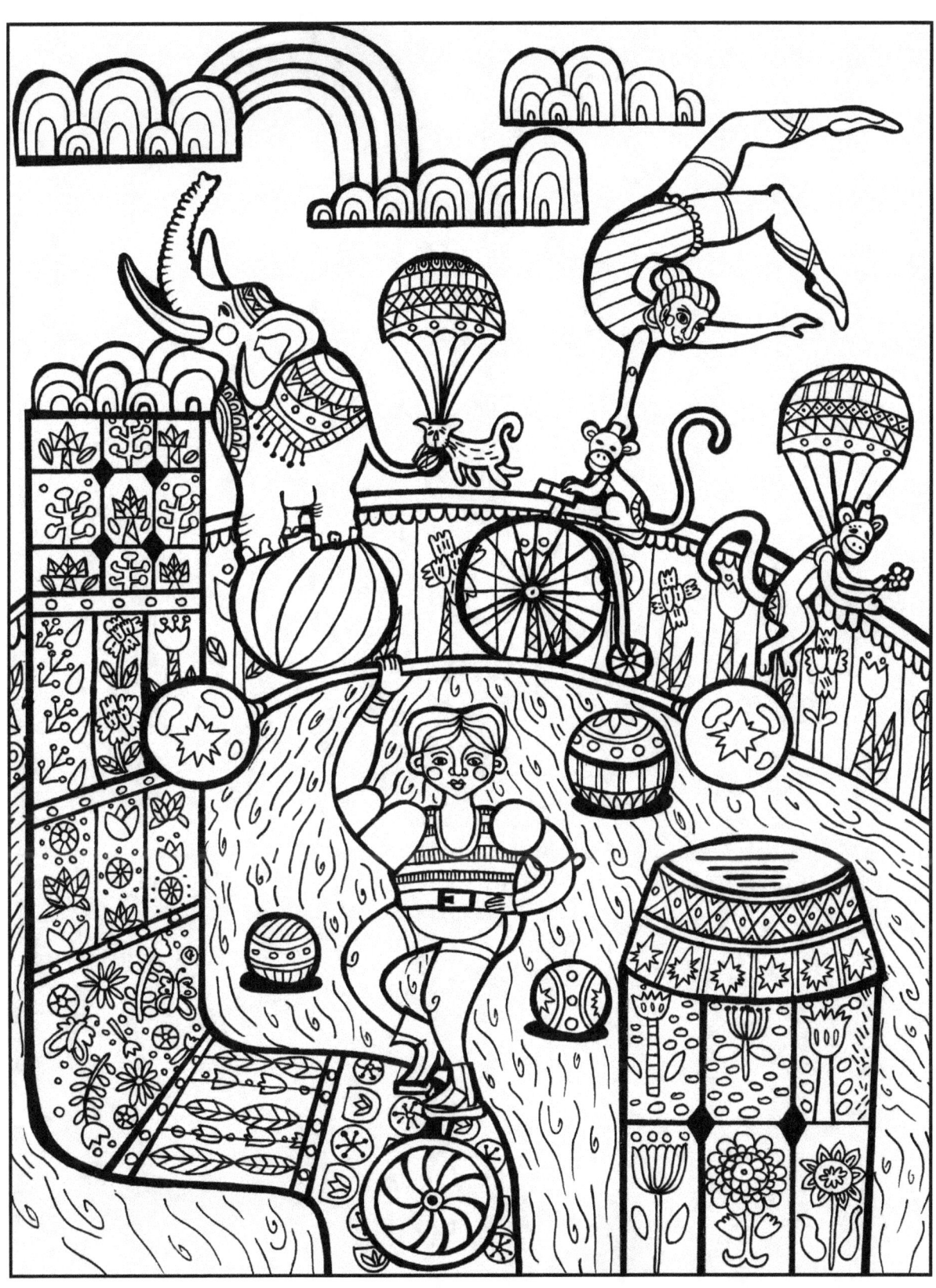

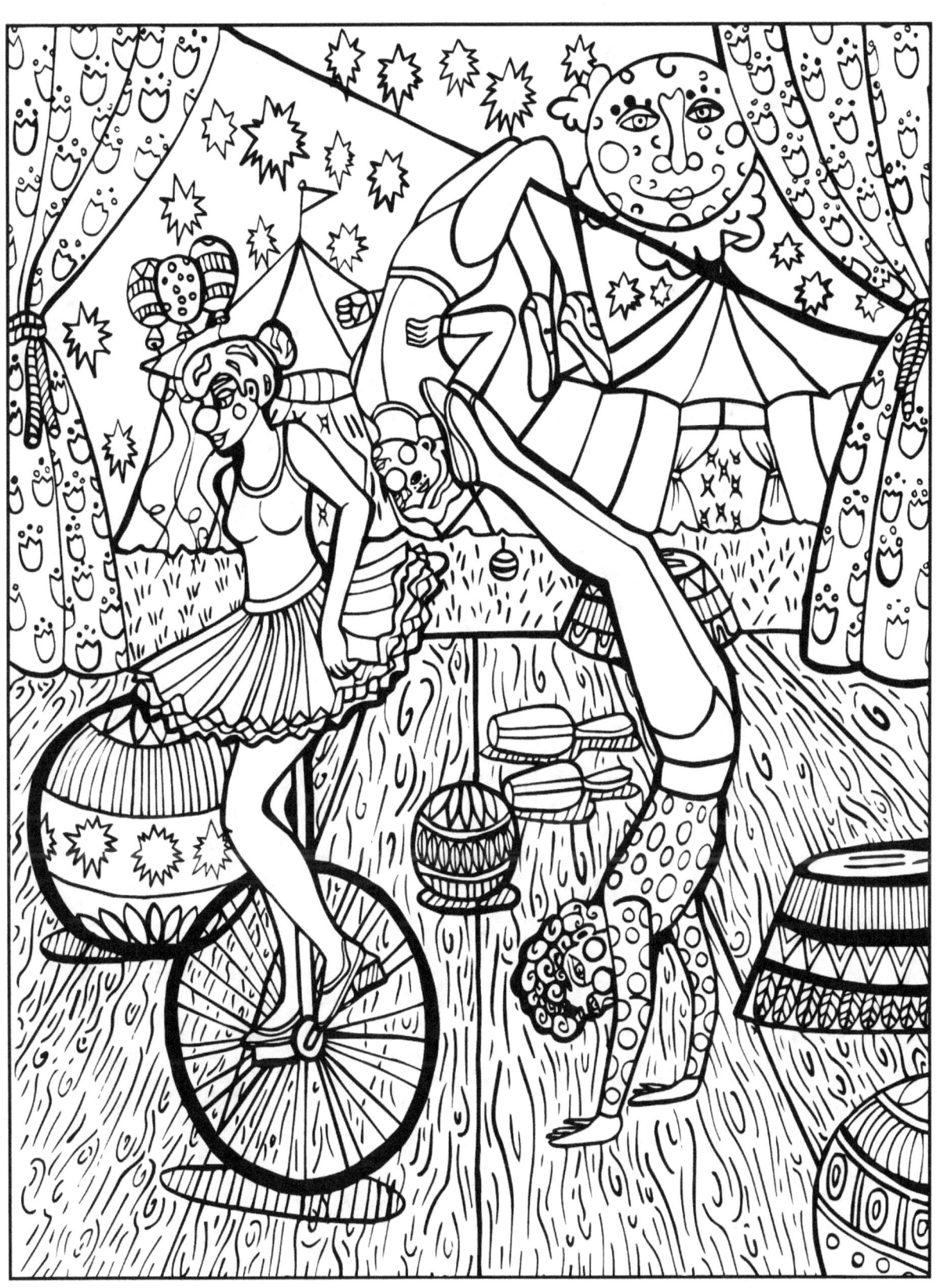

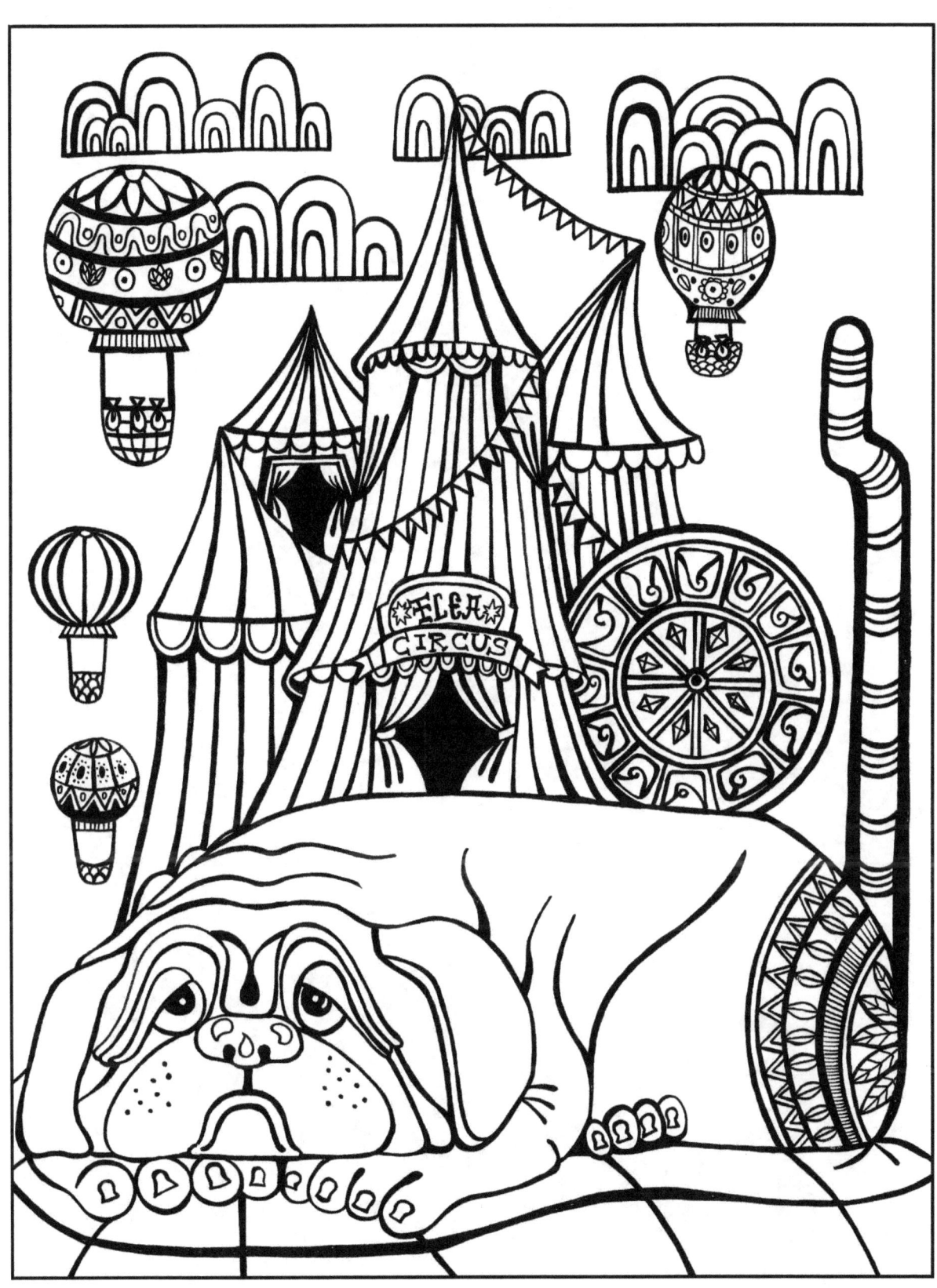

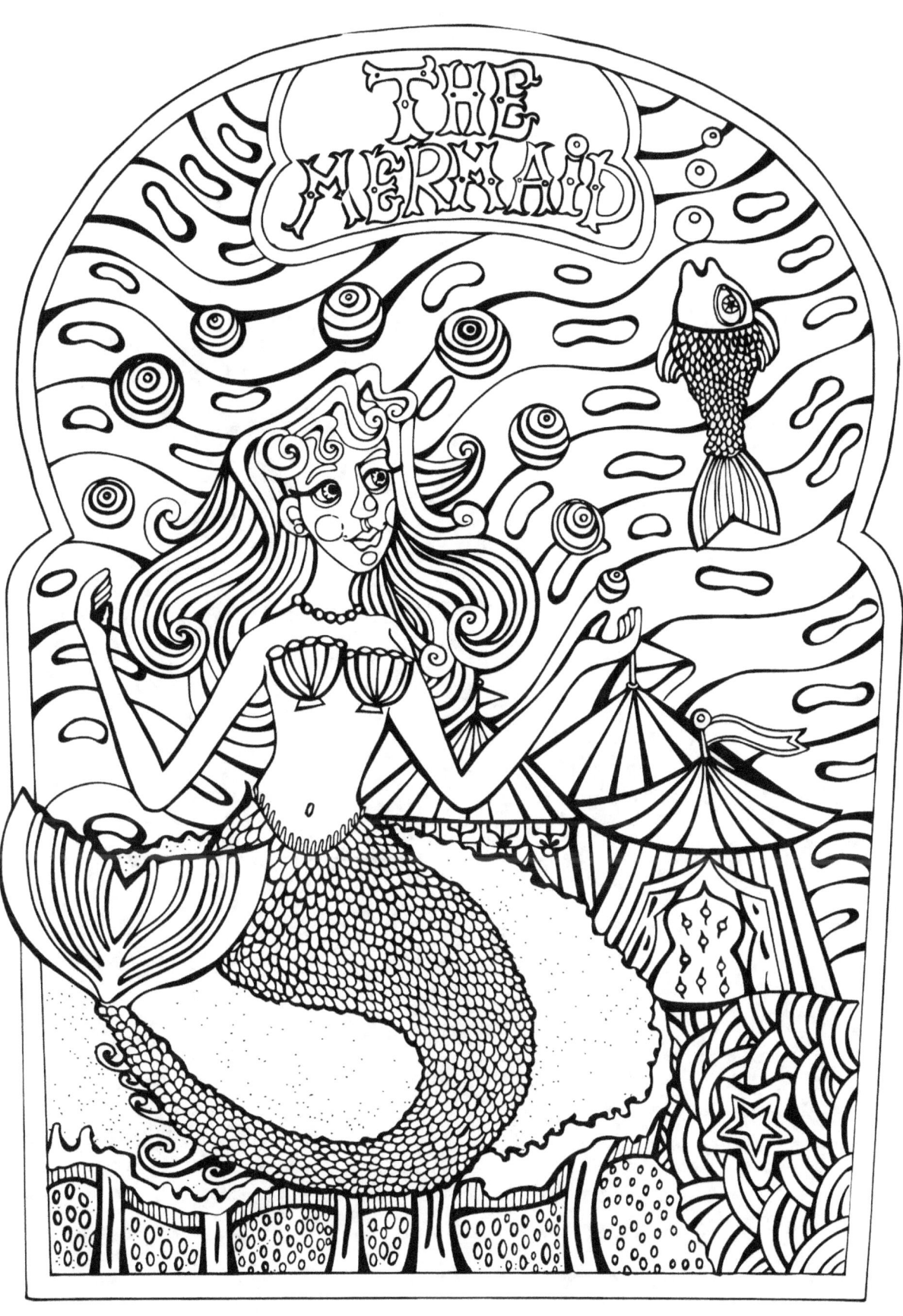

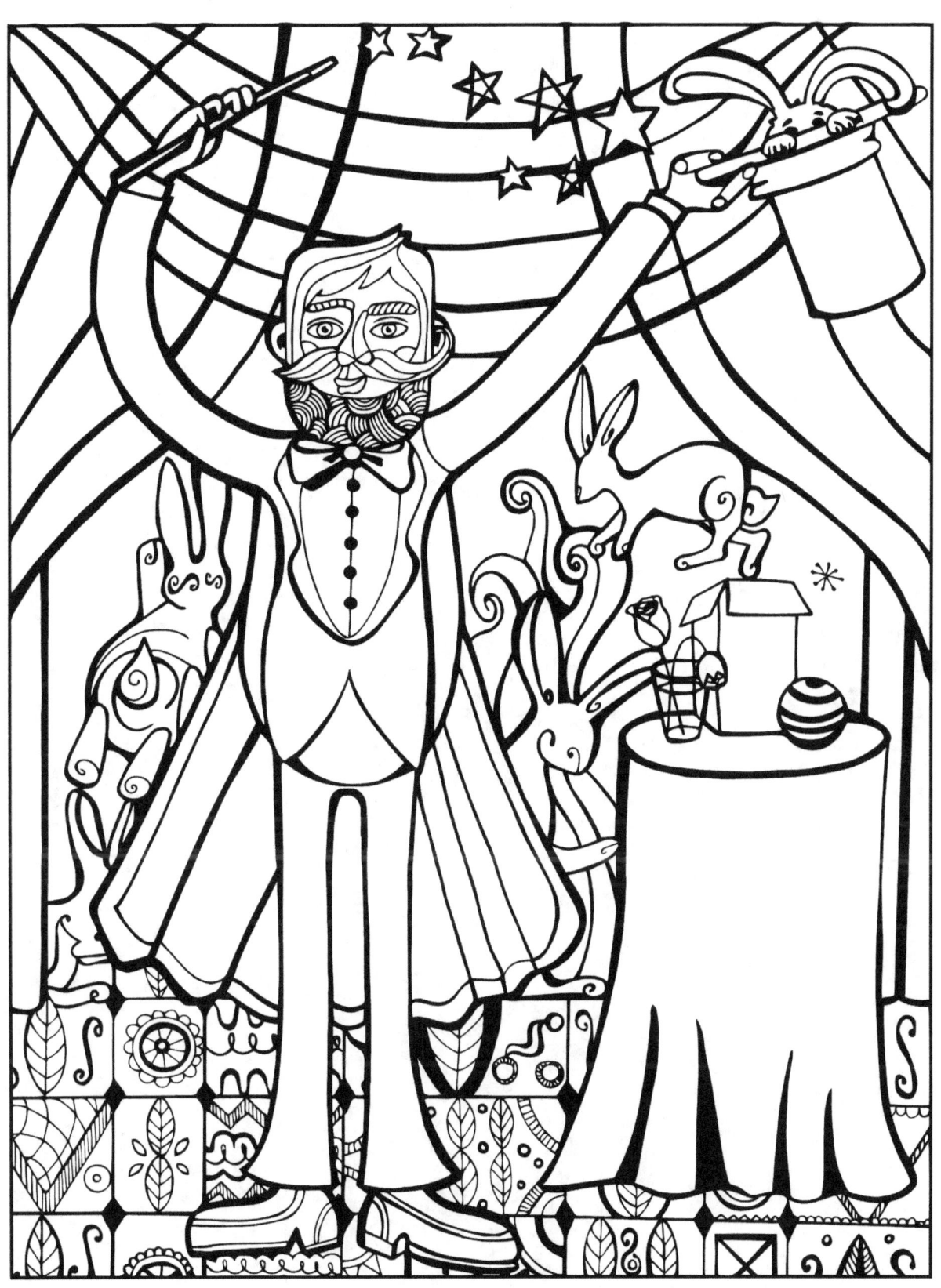

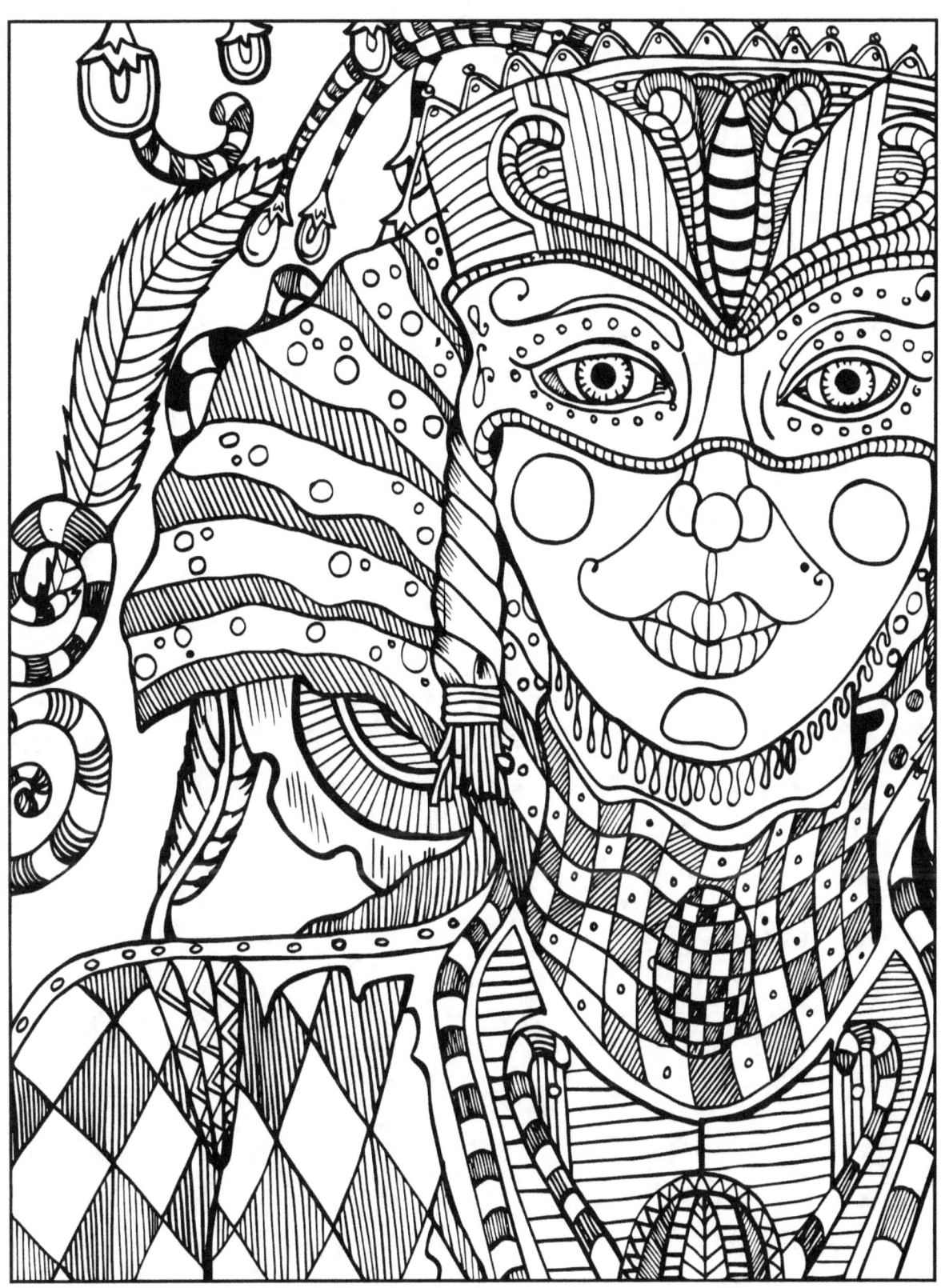

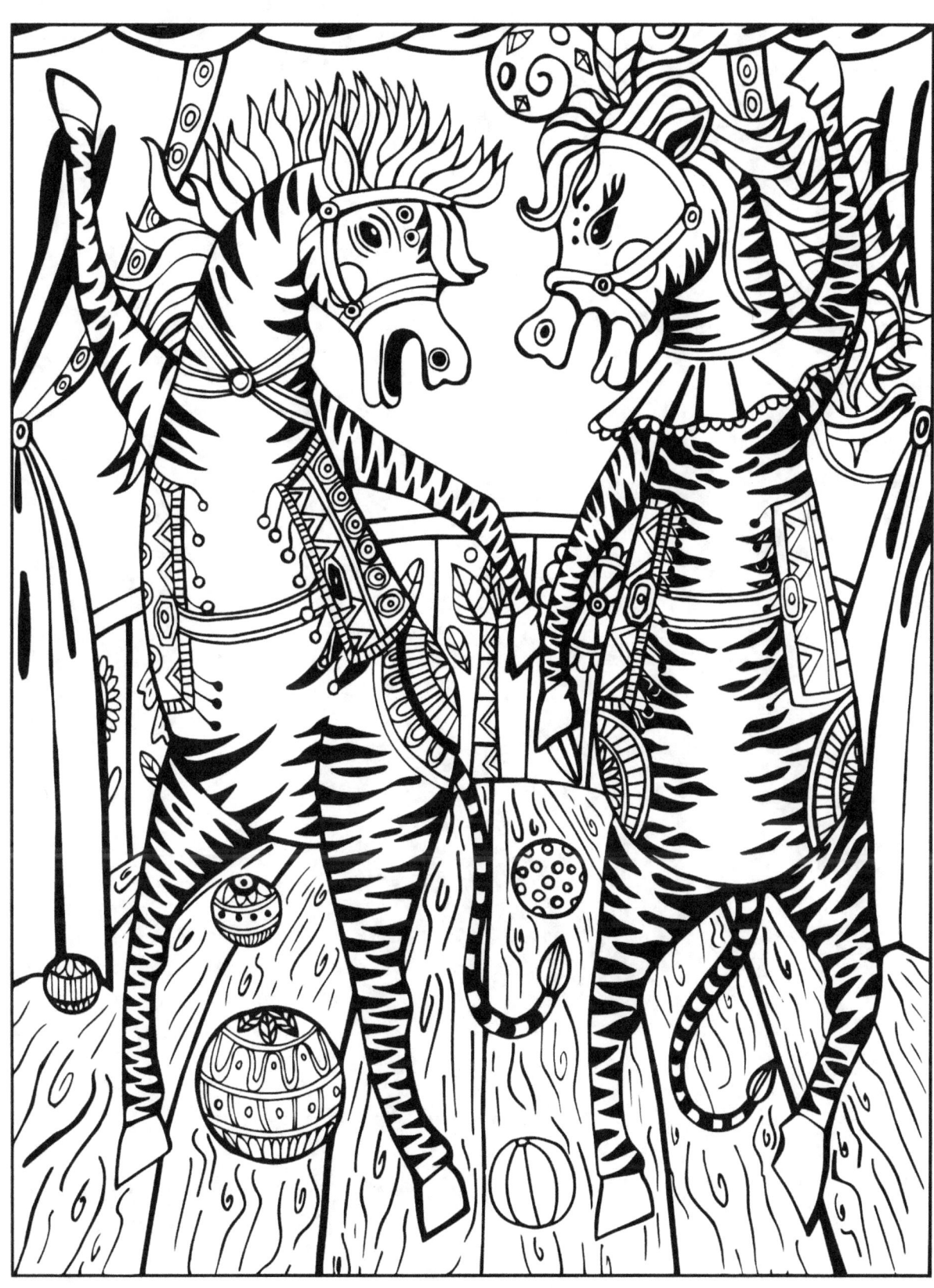

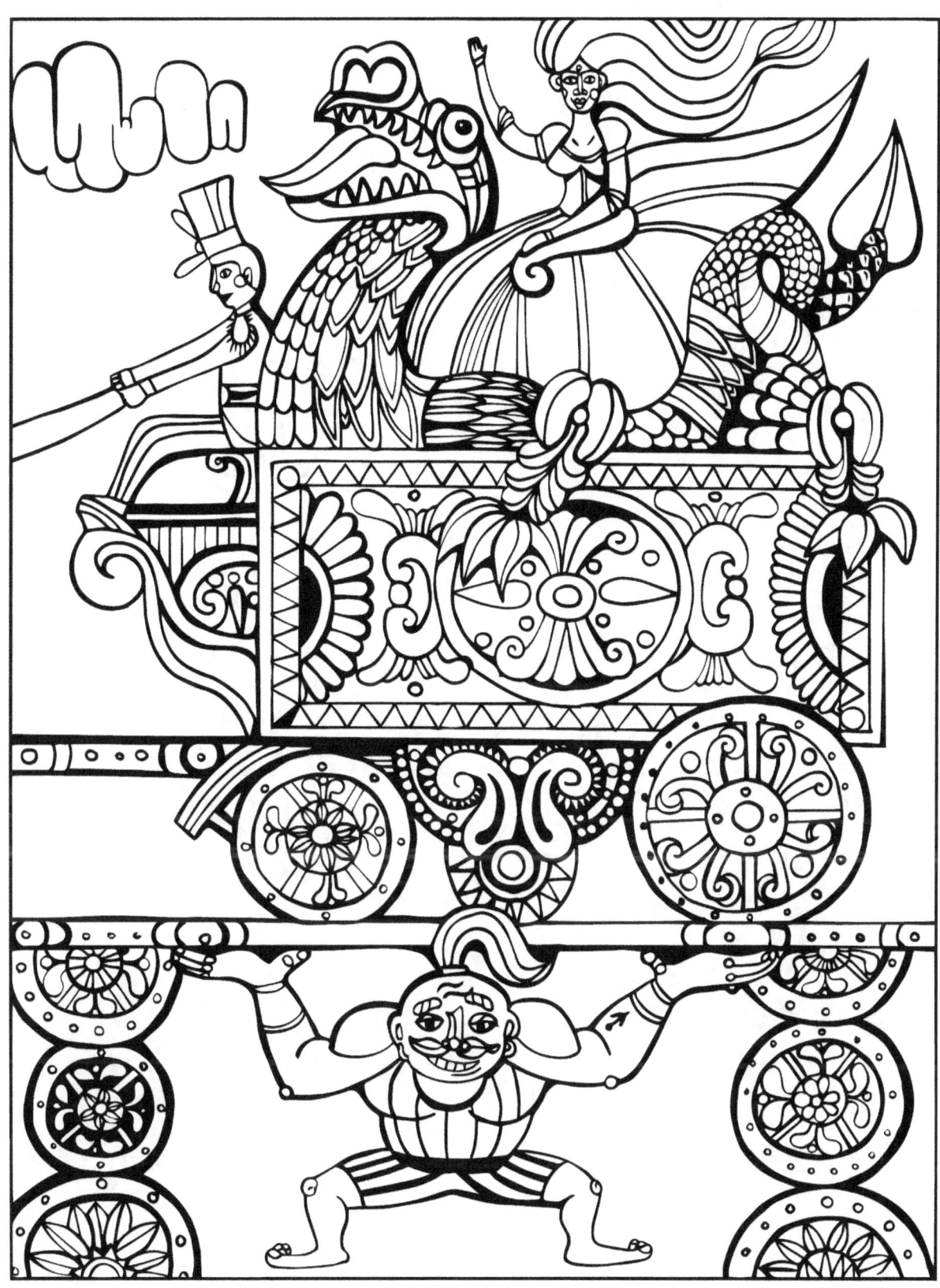

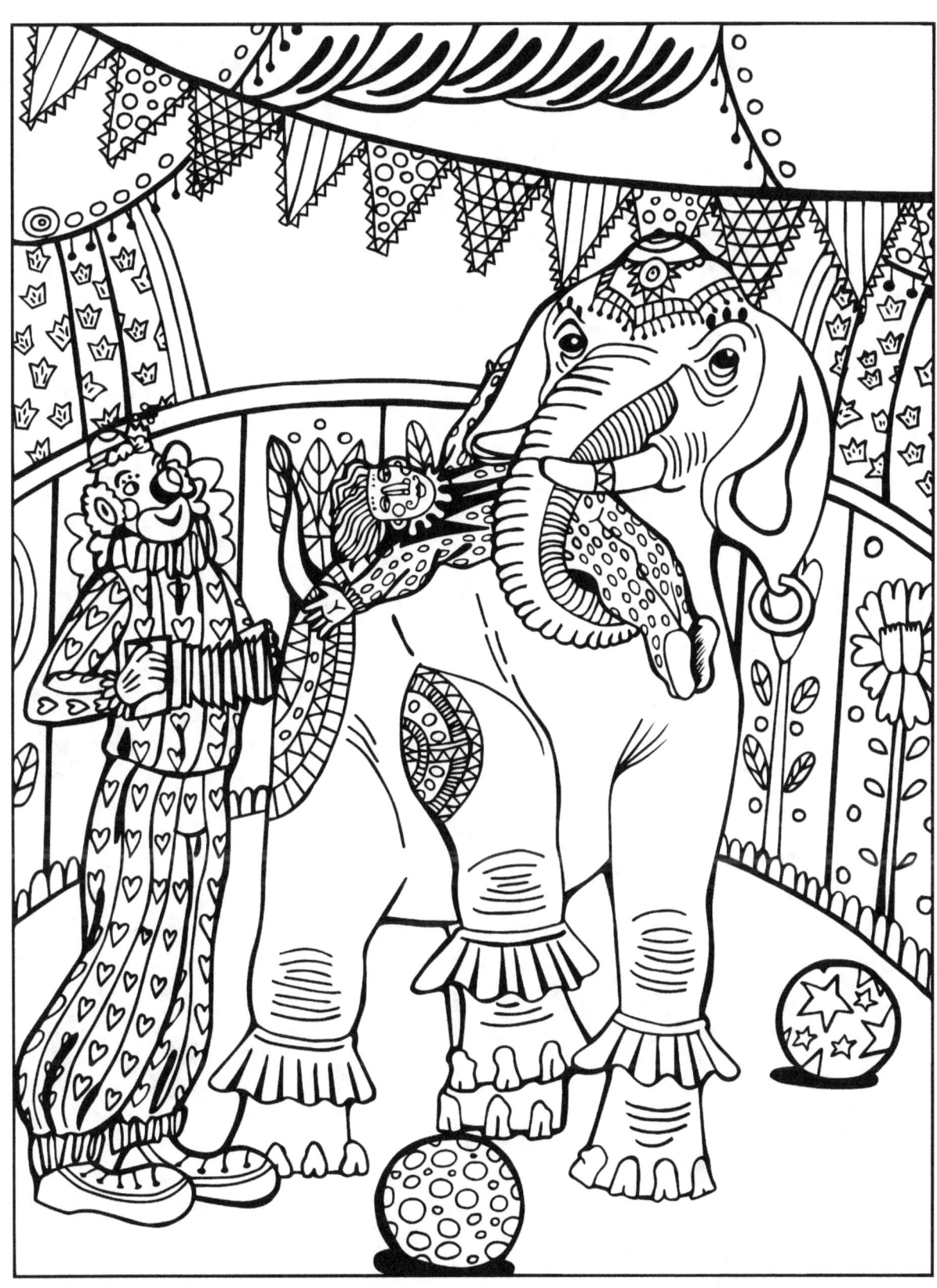

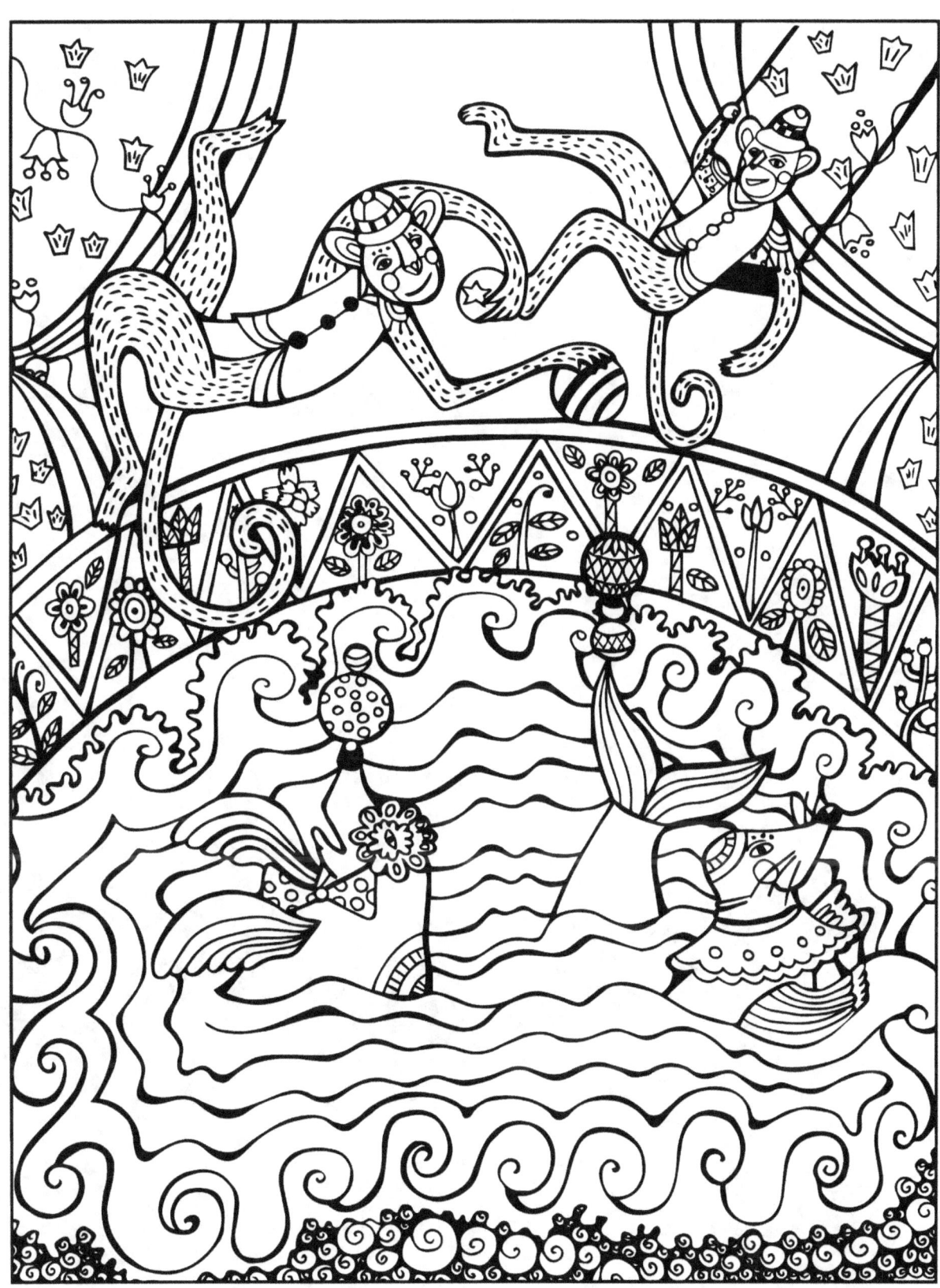

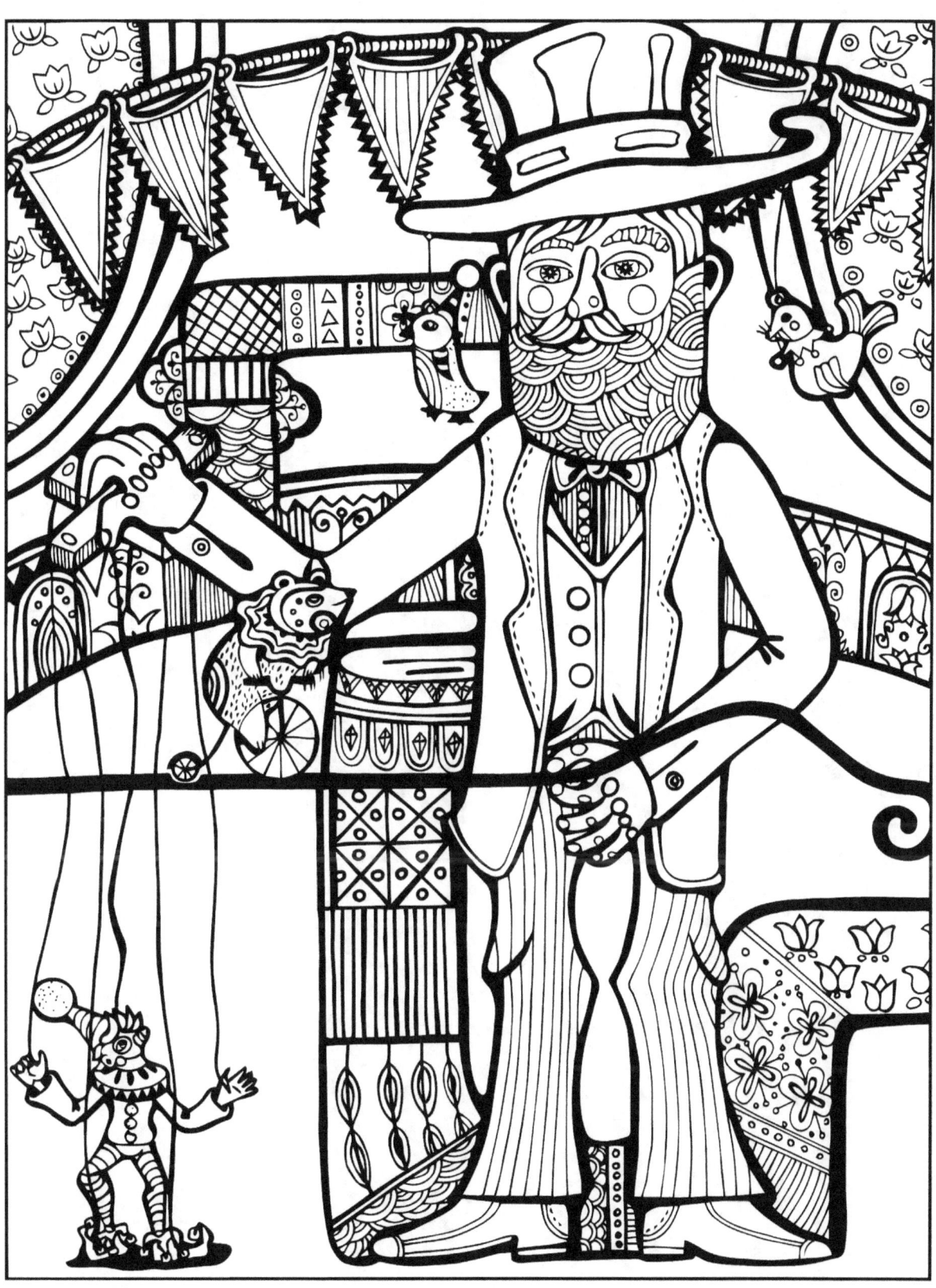

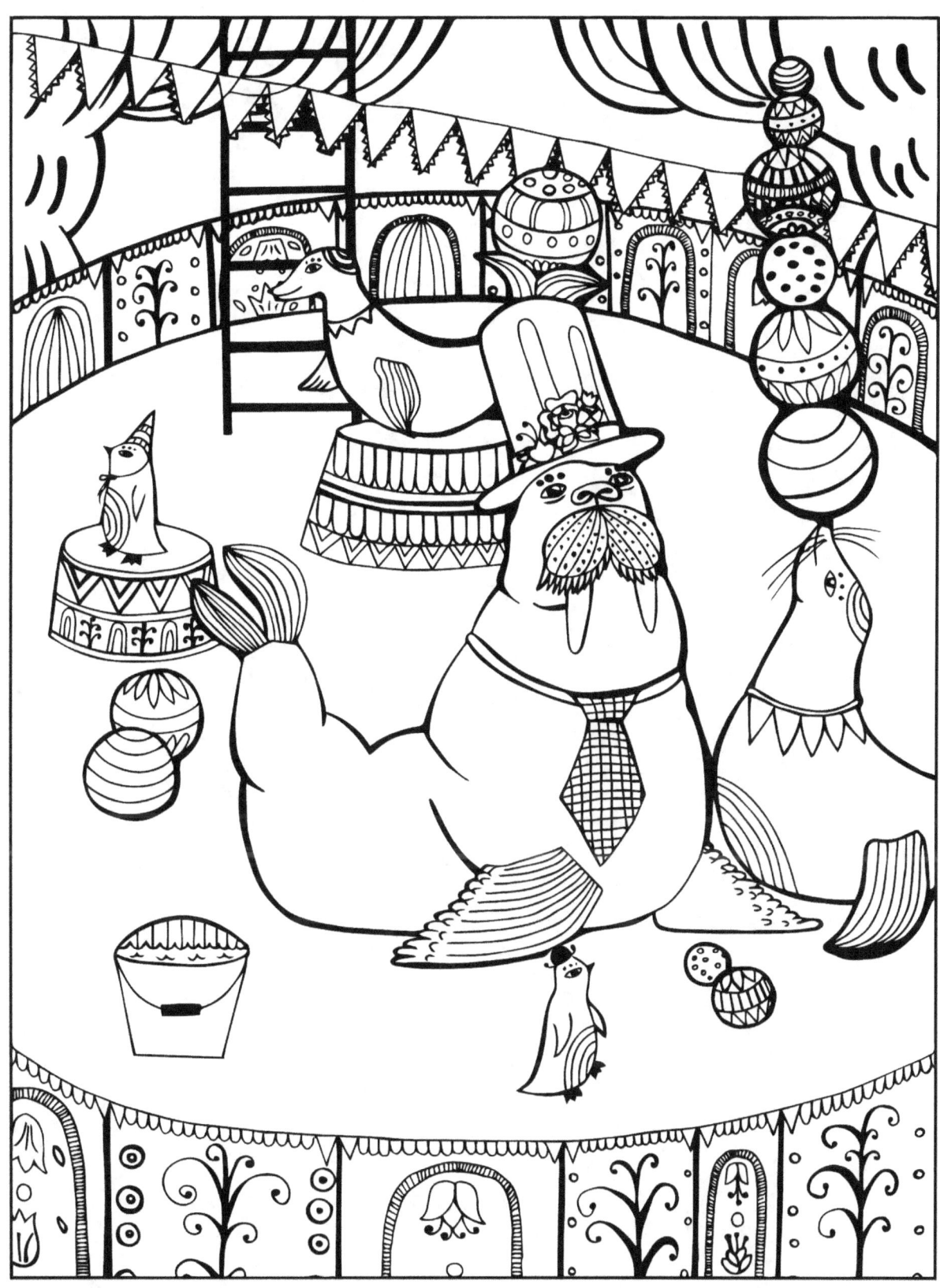

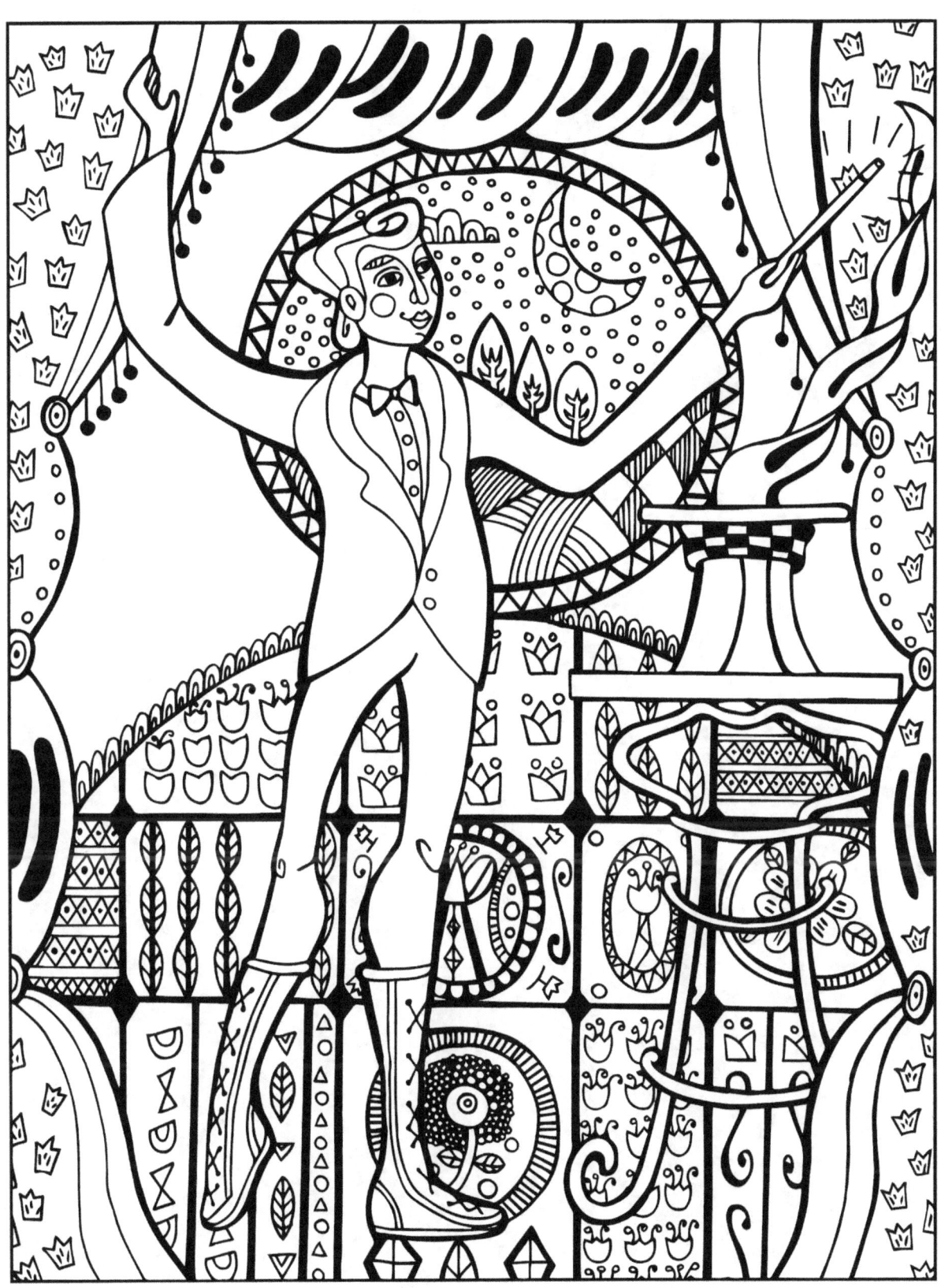

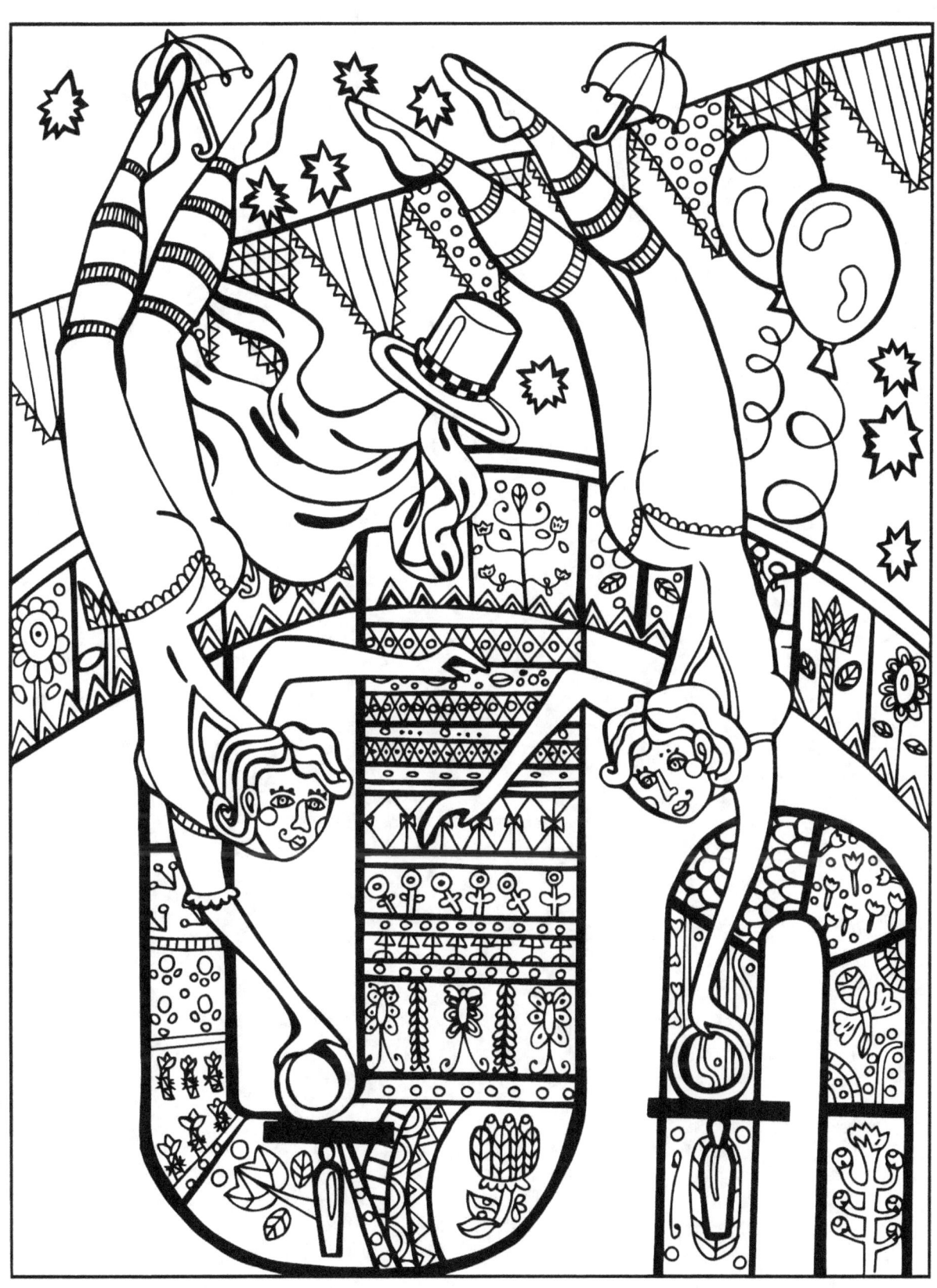

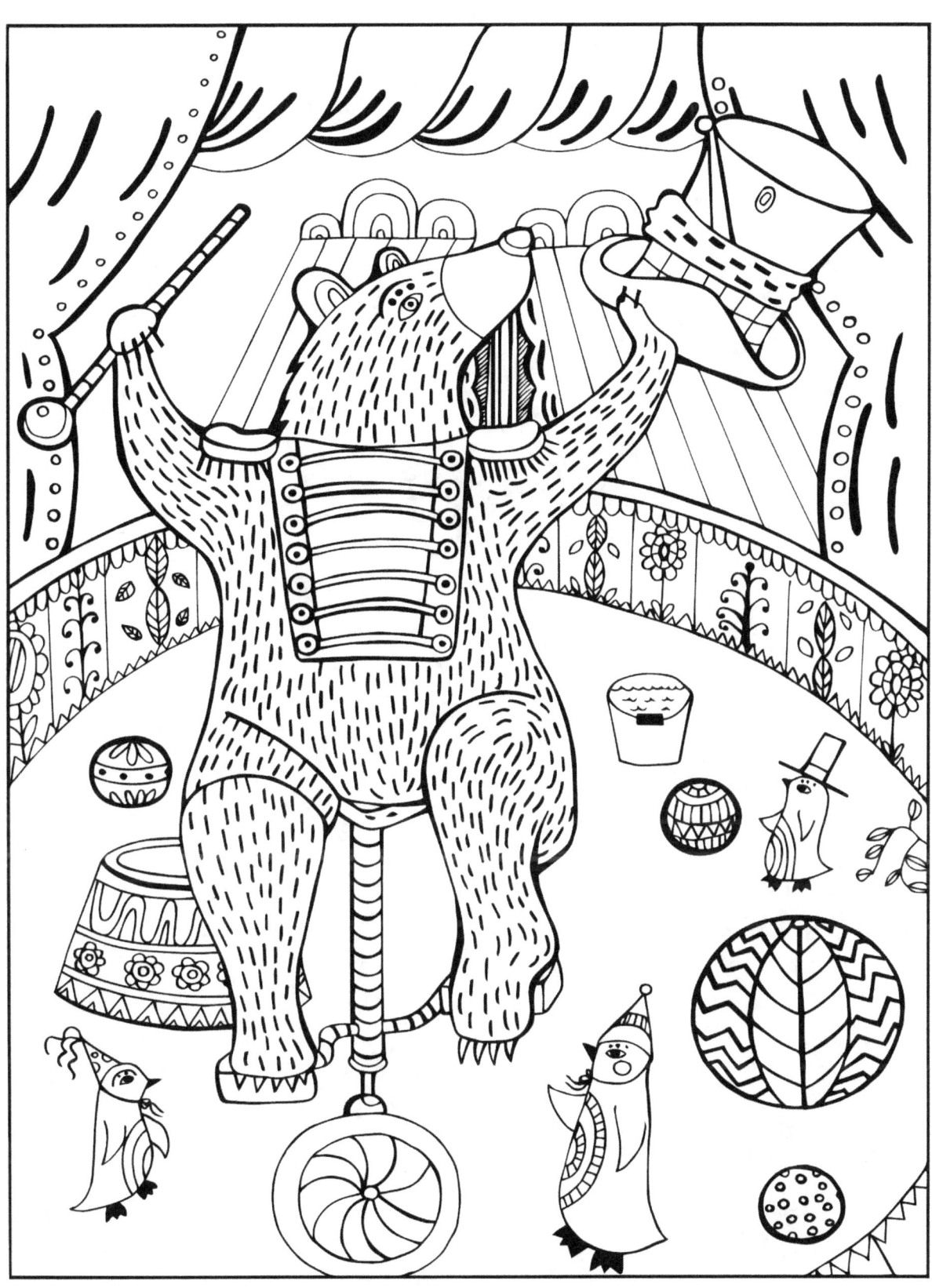

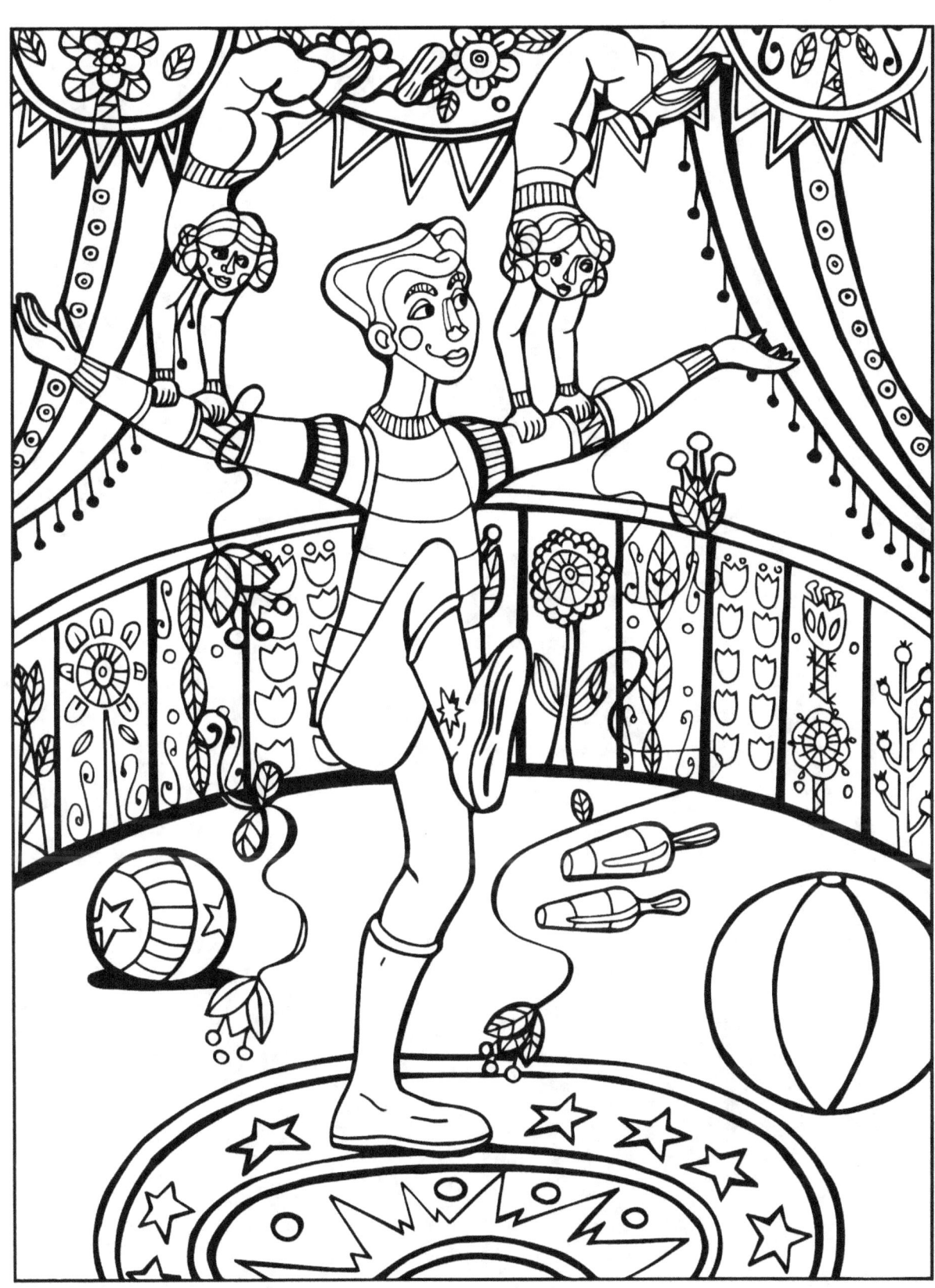

Other Adult Coloring Books Available Only At Amazon

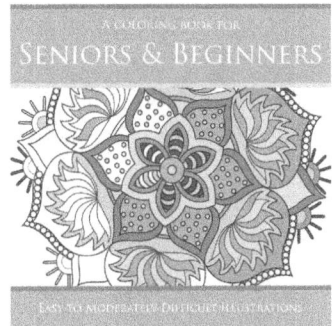

This is a coloring book for anyone wanting a simplified and relaxing coloring experience. The benefits of coloring should be available to people at all skill levels. Excessive complexity and microscopic spaces make many best-selling adult coloring books unsuitable for the vast majority of seniors and beginners.

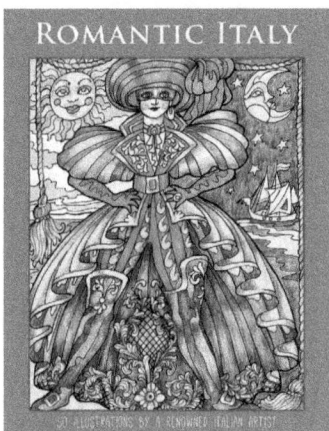

The beautiful illustrations in this book will virtually transport you to this magical land. They will: invite you to join the ostentatious merriment of Carnevale in Venice; reacquaint you with the classic fables of childhood including Pinocchio, Cinderella, Sleeping Beauty and Peter Pan; take you into enchanting gardens filled with flowers, birds and butterflies; escort you through forests filled with animals, castles, and bridges; immerse you among the creatures of the undersea world; and show you classic designs used to make Italy's incomparable "Maiolica" ceramics. "Romantic Italy" is unique among coloring books in that each and every illustration was drawn by hand.

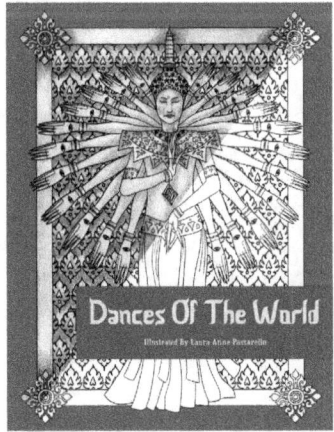

Dance has been an important form of cultural expression throughout human history. This book captures the unique aspects of traditional dance across many of the diverse cultures of the world. Its 36 illustrations will transport you on a virtual journey spanning the Americas, the Caribbean Islands, Europe, Asia and the islands of the Pacific Ocean. In addition to well-known dances such as France's can can and Argentina's tango, you'll find exotic dances such as odissi of India and the aspara of Cambodia. And, the dancers' festive costumes represent invitations for the application of abundant color.

www.ingramcontent.com/pod-product-compliance
Lightning Source LLC
Chambersburg PA
CBHW080947170526
45158CB00008B/2404